SALES
GROWTH

Insights from leading sales executives

| Thomas Baumgartner | Homayoun Hatami | Jon Vander Ark |

McKinsey&Company

Editors: Geoffrey Lewis and Jonathan Turton

Design and layout: Downey Drouin

www.mckinsey.com

Contents

Acknowledgments 1

An agenda for growth by 110 sales executives 5

Executive summary 11

Part one: Find growth before your competitors do 19

1. Look 10 quarters ahead 23

    Surf the trends 25

    Invest ahead of demand 28

    Make it a way of life 31

    Interview: William J. Teuber, Jr., EMC 36

2. Mine growth beneath the surface 39

    Find the pockets of growth 41

    Look beyond sales 46

    Keep it easy for the sales team 48

    Interview: Alejandro Munoz, DuPont Pioneer 51

Part two: Sell the way your customers want 55

3. Master multichannel sales 61

    Blend remote sales and field sales 65

    Integrate online and offline 67

    Orchestrate direct and indirect channels 68

Bring service channels into the fold 69

Interview: Gregory Lee, Samsung 73

4. Innovate direct sales 77

Engage customers early 78

Bring your expertise to the table 81

Pursue new prospects relentlessly 87

5. Invest in partners for mutual profit 91

Manage partners as an extension of
your sales force 95

Confront channel conflict head-on 102

Interview: Stu L. Levenick, Caterpillar 106

Part three: Soup up your sales engine 111

6. Tune sales operations for growth 115

Give sales teams more time to sell 119

Use sales operations to customers' benefit 124

7. Build a technological advantage in sales 129

Arm the sales team 131

Enable channel partners 134

Improve the customer experience 137

Interview: Frank van Veenendaal, Salesforce.com 142

Part four: It's all about you and your people 147

8. Manage performance for growth 153

    Coach rookies into rainmakers 158

    Set the tempo of performance 160

    It's not just about pay 162

    Interview: Mario Weiss, Würth 164

9. Build sales DNA 169

    Create a culture for the long term 172

    Give middle managers a starring role 175

    Put together the A-team 177

10. Growth starts at the very top 183

    Challenge the status quo 185

    Galvanize your team 186

    Be the role model for change 187

    Demand results, results, results! 189

    Interview: Hubert Patricot, Coca-Cola Enterprises 191

About the authors 195

Index 197

Acknowledgments

In any undertaking such as this there are, of course, many many people we must thank for their immense help.

First and foremost, we would like to show our gratitude and admiration to the sales executives we interviewed. Their individual stories and those of their organizations form the blueprint for sales growth that we have tried to capture here. Their insights and courage inspired us to write this book. We cannot name them here, but they all know who they are. They were generous with their time and ideas. We thank each and every one of them.

To convert stories into a book is not so straightforward. It was made possible only thanks to the friends on our editorial board: Par Edin, Roland John, Sunil Rayan, Maria Valdivieso de Uster, and Jennifer Wickland. It is hard to describe the dedication this team displayed. Between them they have helped craft every page and contributed enormously to our thinking. Of course we could also not have written this book without the help of our editors Geoffrey Lewis and Jonathan Turton. They helped push us to focus on "what's new," encouraged us to write a book of stories, not of prescriptive frameworks, and we think made the book an enjoyable read.

We benefited from substantive contributions from a group of colleagues who were, in effect, our co-authors for some of the chapters: Manish Goyal and Maryanne Hancock (chapter 2), Eric Harmon (chapter 7), Olivia Nottebohm (chapter 6), Darren Pleasance (chapter 5), Michael Viertler (chapter 3), Ben Vonwiller (chapter 9), Wesley Walden (chapter 5), and Lareina Yee (chapter 4).

This book is based on interviews and stories. More than 110 interviews were conducted by us and by other members of the McKinsey & Company sales practice. These interviews underpin the foundations of all that we have written, and thus this book would not have been possible without the support of our many colleagues around the world who talked to the sales executives. We are grateful to all of them: Whit Alexander, Guillaume Bonniol, Kevin Chan, Alexander Dahlke, Roxane Divol, Achim Dünnwald, Ben Fletcher, Tjark Freundt, Marcus Hohmann, Jay Jubas, Hans-Werner Kaas, Yongah Kim, Jan-Christoph Köstring, Rene Langen, Richard Lee, Oskar Lingqvist, Monica McGurk, Christophe Meunier, Jean-Christophe Mieszala, Kiyoshi Miura, Laura Moran, John Murnane, Joseph Myers, Georg Nederegger, Christian Pawlu, Andrew Pickersgill, Rohit Razden, Hugo Sarrazin, Markus Schachner, Olivier Sibony, Guil Silva, Chris Simon, Tom Stephenson, Angus Sullivan, Josh Sullivan, Jan Thiel, Andreas Tobler, Steve Truxal, Jochen Ulrich, Jim Wartinbee, Dominik Wee, Jack Welch, and Fanfei Wu.

We also would like to thank those colleagues who reviewed sections of this book and shared their specific expertise with us, especially Philipp Barmettler, Duarte Braga, Guillaume de Roquemarel, David Edelman, Christoph Erbenich, Laura Furmanski, Josh Leibowitz, Jigar Patel, Candace Lun Plotkin, Sara Prince, Jacob Staun, and Rebecca Wahl.

We also benefited from support from Beth Cobert, David Court, Peter Dahlstrom, Tom French, and Marc Singer. They gave us helpful advice at the inception of our project.

Our publishing team turned this effort from a lengthy electronic file into an actual book. Our thanks to Downey Drouin, our designer, and Susanna Eiber, who coordinated the project. Petra Bender, Kari McNamara, and Emmanuelle Tranchant deserve special appreciation for helping us organize ourselves to write this book.

And finally, we would like to thank our spouses Sabina, Cybèle, and Amy for their patience, encouragement, and love over the year we worked intensely on writing this book. We are grateful to them every day.

We have thanked a lot of people. All played their part in writing this book but any errors remain of course our own. It has been a privilege to hear so many great sales stories, and an even greater one to be able to pass them on to you.

An agenda for growth by 110 sales executives

In the summer of 2010, McKinsey & Company hosted a series of discussions with a small group of senior sales executives from large companies, many of which are global leaders in their fields. The world was starting to recover from the economic downturn, so inevitably the topic of conversation was how best to renew growth. The sales leaders shared how they were driving and sustaining growth at this time of challenge and opportunity.

"It is all about focus and timing," said one. "Over the past ten years we've been through two major recessions and we've reviewed what worked and what didn't. We think what's most important for sustainable sales performance is getting a perspective of where the market is headed." By identifying emerging opportunities and systematically attacking them before competitors, her company planned to gain half a dozen percentage points of market share and expected margins to hit record levels.

"Less is more," declared another sales leader. "Customers in our industry are increasingly sensitive about how much time they have to spend meeting with sales reps. They want fewer, more productive interactions. And they value the ease of use and the lower cost of the Web. We've listened and have radically raised our game online—both in sales and service. We've seen a 15 to 20 percent increase in sales, while cutting the cost-to-serve by more than 15 percent."

For a third sales executive, the message from the crisis was clear: "Companies must transform or die. After the crisis we got rid of all types of waste and addressed quality in our sales process." This lean program in her sales back office reduced overall costs by 20 percent. "We then put most of the money into new collaborative tools for our own sales teams and our partners—a far cry from our legacy CRM programs, which never really worked," she added. Again, the results were impressive: the company saw a 15 percent uptake in sales and a big boost in morale in the sales organization.

Another sales leader told us, "It's all about the coaching and support you give your sales staff." He explained that, in the depth of the crisis, he had launched a series of pilots to improve individual sales reps' performance, with a particular focus on hands-on coaching. Every morning the managers would run through that day's priorities and brainstorm solutions to any challenges. Despite a difficult market, total contract value per week rose by 30 percent and customer satisfaction improved by half a dozen percentage points. "Perhaps more important for long-term success," he said, "our sales people felt more satisfied with their work."

Four sets of questions emerged over the course of these discussions, all focused on how sales executives in large companies can drive and sustain growth:

- How do we get to growth opportunities before competitors do—be it through capturing trends, or finding pockets of growth in existing markets?

- How can the organization use multiple channels to serve customers of different sizes and with different needs—and how can it optimize direct and indirect channels?

- How can companies use sales operations and technology as true engines of growth?

- How does a company drive near-term growth while building capabilities for the long term?

Underpinning all these questions—and of course of utmost relevance to senior sales executives—is what sales leaders themselves should do differently.

This book explores how senior sales executives around the world are tackling these issues. We at McKinsey & Company have a perspective based on our work advising large corporations on their top-line growth, and from our proprietary databases of business and retail customers' perception of their sales experience. But for this book, we wanted to go back to the source. We went and spoke to world-class sales executives to find out how they are grappling with these challenges and to gather real-world lessons and ideas.

Starting in June 2010, we interviewed more than 110 senior sales executives from global companies across industries that have a track record of outperforming their peers in revenue and margin growth over the past five years (Exhibit 1).[1]

---

1 Public filings.

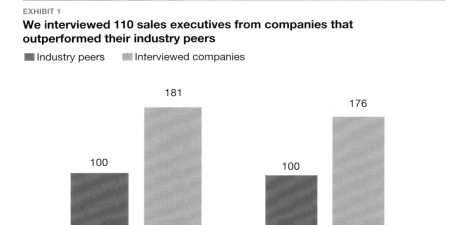

EXHIBIT 1
We interviewed 110 sales executives from companies that outperformed their industry peers

■ Industry peers   ▨ Interviewed companies

181

176

100

100

Revenue growth
2004-09 (index)

EBITDA growth
2004-09 (index)

We chose to interview sales executives in large companies (averaging $30 billion revenues, $44 billion market cap., and 80,000 employees), because the bigger you are, the harder it is to outgrow your competitors, and the harder it is to do it again and again.

We talked to companies across 10 industry sectors: telecommunications, high tech, media, industrial manufacturing, basic materials, travel and logistics, financial services, healthcare and pharmaceuticals, consumer goods, and retail. Roughly half the companies we interviewed faced the complexity of selling to both business and consumer markets, a third were purely business-focused, and the remainder entirely consumer-focused.

Almost two-thirds of the sales executives we interviewed led global sales organizations, with an average revenue mix of

40 percent in North America; 40 percent in Europe, the Middle East, and Africa; and 20 percent in Asia and the rest of the world. To ensure a global and local mix of perspectives, we also spoke to leaders in charge of sales regions and major countries and made a particular effort to interview sales executives focused solely on emerging markets.

We have tried to make this book a blueprint for sales growth—drafted by sales executives for sales executives. To share the lessons we heard, we decided to tell a series of stories, offering real-world examples rather than frameworks, because we feel that these stories are more powerful (and more enjoyable to read).

Collectively, these anecdotes and case studies capture the experiences of leading sales executives as they have rethought how to find growth, how to capture it, and how to build the capabilities to keep growing in the future. We did not try to be exhaustive, so this book is not a guide to everything a head of sales should do. We rather decided to focus on "what's new" and interesting as we tried to portray the success of these 110 sales executives in driving growth.

This book is a record of experimentation and innovation and, in some cases, courage. We hope it provides you with a set of interesting ideas that can be applied in your company as you pursue sales growth.

Executive summary

This book sets out a blueprint for sales growth. It is based on the experiences of some of the world's most successful sales executives and how they met the challenges that large global companies encounter in their quest for growth. Four big themes emerged from our interviews with these leaders, which provide the structure for this book.

Part one: Find growth before your competitors do

It is not always obvious where growth lies. Companies need to be prepared to search for new business in different ways. The sales executives we spoke to look ahead to where tomorrow's growth will emerge and look below the surface of today's markets to find hidden opportunities. Specifically, they:

- **Look 10 quarters ahead.** Excellent sales organizations scan the horizon to discover growth opportunities. They do this by closely monitoring economic, technological, and behavioral market trends and they invest in advance to build the capacity to capture the growth. They not only dedicate resources to discovering future sales, they embed the forward-looking mindset throughout their organizations.

- **Mine growth beneath the surface.** Taking a microscope to markets can reveal enormous differences in the growth potential within a given region or segment; even mature markets can contain surprising pockets of growth. Uncovering "micro-markets" requires strong data analytics capabilities—exploiting them depends on turning the strategy into a simple message for the front line.

Part two: Sell the way your customers want

We all believe that price, product, and service are what customers prize most because that's what they say in surveys. But our analysis of actual behavior shows that the sales experience is equally important—and critical to building loyalty. World-class sales leaders know that they have to work hard to give customers the selling experience they want across the channels they want. They also know that, increasingly, they need to engage the same customers across different channels. They develop integrated multichannel strategies and ensure that each channel is delivering to its full potential. Three important ways to keep customers not just satisfied, but delighted with every interaction, emerged from our interviews:

- **Master multichannel sales.** With so many channels to choose from, it's easy to lose contact with customers—and even entire segments—as they move about. The same customer who meets with your major-accounts manager is also placing orders by phone and scouring the Web for deals and information about you and your competitors. At the same time, you need to know that dealers, retailers, and other channel partners deliver great customer experience, too. To provide a seamless sales experience across those channels is certainly challenging. Even the best sales leaders have struggled. But they have mastered multichannel sales with consistent approaches for blending remote and field sales, integrating online and offline channels, orchestrating direct and indirect sales teams, and even using service as a sales channel. The permutations are almost endless, but robust multichannel processes will ensure customers stay happy.

- **Innovate direct sales.** The most successful direct sales forces—whether in B2B or B2C—have taken customer experience to a new level, making their direct sales organizations a vital source of insight into how the customer can succeed in his or her business. They engage customers early, often well before any sales pitches. They make sure that the customer has access to the right people with the right knowledge in the most cost-effective and timely way. Finally, the top direct sales teams are not afraid to innovate in search of growth. Even for the biggest suppliers in the most highly-developed markets there are always new ways to land new customers and clients.

- **Invest in partners for mutual profit.** Companies can no longer afford to treat third-party partners as a second-class channel. In many cases, a partner is the best or only way to reach the fastest-growing markets. How do you make sure channel partners represent your product the way you would—and that the customer is getting the experience you want associated with your brand? How do you handle the age-old problem of channel conflict? The philosophy is simple: treat them as an extension of the sales force, help them with their own bottom lines, and set clear guidelines for channel conflict. Making it happen requires finesse.

Part three: Soup up your sales engine

Sales leaders can't deliver on all the dimensions outlined in the first two sections without the right capabilities in the back office. An efficient and effective sales support operation is critically important for supporting the direct sales force and channel partners. It must be responsive and capable—and it can't be too costly. Increasingly, this means getting technology right, another perennial struggle that the best sales organizations have learned how to tackle.

- **Tune sales operations for growth.** Improving sales operations is critical both to growth and profitability. Sales operations typically represent one of the best opportunities for SG&A improvement, and leading sales organizations have stripped hundreds of millions of dollars of waste out of sales processes. But they have also remembered that sales operations are an important contributor to customer experience and the effectiveness of the sales force.

- **Build a technological advantage in sales.** Sales technology continues to evolve and the best sales organizations have learned to make their investments a central enabler of sales success. Technology helps sales leaders gain an advantage over competitors, arming account managers with killer insights to target customers or enabling better integration with channel partners and, increasingly, improving the customer experience through digital channels.

Part four: It's all about you and your people

For all the talk of growth analysis, channels, and technology, we all know that leadership in sales is ultimately about people. The sales leaders we spoke to were keenly aware of this and invest significant time in ensuring they get the best out of their staff. To do this they:

- **Manage performance for growth.** Sustainable performance management is far more than working out the variable part of compensation. The best sales organizations invest enormous energy in coaching rookies into stars, they set the right tempo for reporting and intervention, and they know what motivates the sales force beyond just money. They also unleash the capabilities of sales managers, the influential frontline leaders who can really make things happen in the field.

- **Build sales DNA.** Achieving excellence in sales for a couple of quarters is great, but to be world-class companies must have sales growth embedded in their genes. Three themes are common to all the organizations we've seen that successfully recode their sales DNA. They create a culture that's fit for the long term. They give middle managers a starring role in pushing the company forward and acting as agents of change. They also focus on creating a crack team rather than just improving individuals' capabilities.

- **Growth starts at the very top.** Sales leaders also know that they have to be at the vanguard of change themselves. They know that growth starts at the top. This means you! Without strong leadership it's virtually impossible to make change stick and any growth program will eventually flounder. World-class sales leaders consistently do four things outstandingly well: they challenge the status quo, they galvanize their team, they role-model change, and they demand results beyond and above everything else.

Sales leaders may ask: "What can I realistically expect from putting in place all these ideas?" The ideas and case stories presented here are not just illustrations of how you should think about sales leadership. They comprise a roadmap to tangible top-line growth and bottom-line improvement. Sales growth programs that are designed and executed successfully often achieve growth of between 10 and 30 percent (on the revenue affected by the program), with increased (or at least no decline in) profitability.

Part one:
Find growth before
your competitors do

Finding growth that lies beyond the fiscal horizon is not the sole responsibility of the CEO or the head of strategy. While growth can come from acquiring new businesses or from launching new product lines, it can also come from sales leaders who develop a sense of where market momentum is moving or where untapped sources of growth lay hidden. They steal the march on competitors and lock in new customers first.

Many of the sales executives we met play a central role in finding growth opportunities for their companies. They make sure their sales organizations have formalized methods—and embedded instincts—to look beyond short-term performance imperatives to find growth. The first two chapters explore these ideas:

Chapter 1: Look 10 quarters ahead is about translating insights from global mega trends like climate change into action at the front line, investing ahead of emerging demand, and even cultivating demand for the products that won't be available for years.

Chapter 2: Mine growth beneath the surface discusses how to develop a granular view of existing markets to see what competitors may routinely overlook. Looking at territories at the zip-code level or at customer segments by industry or by demographic characteristics often reveals untapped pockets of growth—if you find these uncontested opportunities first.

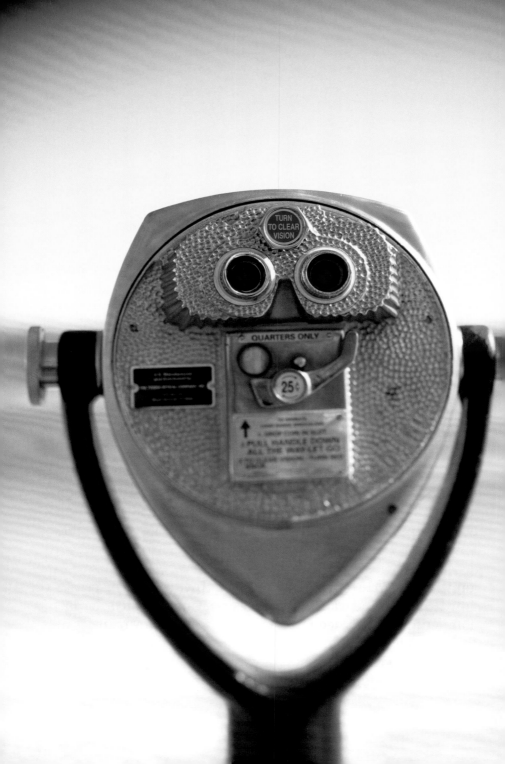

1. Look 10 quarters ahead

"For tomorrow belongs to the people who prepare for it today."

—African proverb

In early 2009, the United States Congress spent weeks drafting the American Recovery and Reinvestment Act. Most companies simply followed the process, praying it would help kick-start sales that had been ravaged by the deep recession. But at one major high-tech equipment company, sales leaders weren't waiting. They knew the legislation would create opportunities for them.

As soon as the bill's outlines came into focus, they got busy planning how to exploit the potential that the new law would provide. They saw that the legislation called for grants and tax rebates to encourage healthcare providers to upgrade IT infrastructure and transition to electronic medical records. This infrastructure included products that the company made.

The sales group swung into action, quickly developing a tailored offering for hospitals. This was not a case of working with product development to launch tailored products. There was no time. Instead, it had to select the suite of products that best fit customers' needs and that fell within the scope of the legislation. They also developed sales collateral that told hospitals exactly how to take advantage of the federal subsidies in the stimulus bill. They quickly met with many hospitals and were able to secure multimillion dollar deals within the first few weeks after the bill was passed.

This is a prime example of forward-looking sales management, an important differentiator of top-performing sales organizations. Certainly, all sales leaders know that they should pay attention to what is happening in the wider world to anticipate changes that could turn into opportunities or threats. But the best follow the example of this company—they make trend analysis a formal part of the sales planning process and, as a result, are perfectly poised to capture the opportunities created by sudden changes in the environment.

Indeed, turning the stimulus package into a coherent, on-the-ground program is just one example of capitalizing on a forward-looking view of the market. Another leading high-tech company's sales leadership continuously monitors economics, consumer behavior, and other forces to identify two or three relevant trends each year, and translates them into concrete sales programs. It develops cross-functional SWAT teams that work with customer account teams to educate customers on the nature of a trend and sell them on its

> Sales leadership continuously monitors economics, consumer behavior, and other forces to identify two or three relevant trends each year.

solution. Whether it's eco-business or cloud computing, by linking sales activities with emerging trends the company has scored breakthrough wins at Fortune 500 customers.

Based on our research and the discussions with the 110 sales executives we interviewed, it is clear that great companies do three interrelated things to capture the benefits of forward thinking:

- **Surf the trends.** Good sales leaders know how to hit monthly and annual sales plans. Great sales leaders tap into the big picture, watching for strategic openings in economic trends or changes in customer sectors and regions. They know these can be real opportunities.

- **Invest ahead of demand.** This might mean making a small investment in analytic capabilities or beefing up the number of frontline sales staff ahead of the emerging trend.

- **Make all this a way of life.** As with the network equipment company, programs that successfully exploited emerging trends were not one-off flukes or lucky bets. Leading sales organizations have a built-in forward perspective and mechanisms to turn that insight into action.

Surf the trends

The high-tech equipment company reacted swiftly to a political change. But developments that create new selling opportunities can come from many sources: technology trends that change consumer shopping patterns or redefine business models, regulatory trends, or political trends (Exhibit 2).[2] To ride these trends, the best sales executives make it their business to know

---

2   Gartner; IDC; Forrester; Recovery.gov; US Climate Network; McKinsey & Company.

EXHIBIT 2

Great sales teams constantly scan the horizon for the next opportunity

	Example trend	Opportunities
Technological	**Cloud computing:** doubling every two years to $80-90 billion by 2014 from $21 billion in 2009	Target small businesses with "pay as you go" model; use proven offering to displace incumbents in enterprise
Political	**Stimulus:** e.g., American Recovery and Reinvestment Act authorizing ~ $800 billion in expenditures in 2009-10	Offer products and services that take advantage of new legislation
Geographical	**Emerging markets:** e.g., 15 countries with annual GDP growth over 7% between 2010 and 2015	Invest sales resources in growing markets to establish incumbent position
Regulatory	**Carbon emission reductions:** e.g., EU targeting 20% reduction by 2020	Go after customers most affected by regulatory changes

what is happening beyond their organizations, their customers, and their industries.

Knowledge is only one part of the equation, though. Top-performing sales organizations have the will and the means to translate macro-shifts into real top-line impact fast. Often, they are able to launch tactical, opportunistic sales programs that deliver differentiated growth in a challenging environment.

For example, as the 2008 financial crisis unfolded, South Korean auto manufacturer Hyundai concluded that economic uncertainty would make consumers skittish about committing to major purchases such as cars. It quickly developed the Hyundai Assurance program that allowed consumers to return their cars with no penalty if they lost their jobs. The program led to Hyundai becoming the only major car manufacturer to increase US sales in 2009.[3]

---

3 Reuters.

Forward-looking sales management can be strategic as well as tactical. The first-mover advantage created by forward-looking sales plans drives sales in areas where competitors have yet to arrive. This enables the pioneer to build share and enjoy high margins, at least for a while. For example, a major IT company that we discuss in detail below has a

> The first-mover advantage created by forward-looking sales plans drives sales in areas where competitors have yet to arrive.

forward-looking sales function whose sole purpose is to accelerate the acceptance of next-generation technology among early adopters to give the company an edge a few years from now.

As we said, sales executives don't just monitor economic trends; there are also mega trends such as climate change that create enormous challenges and opportunities across industries and markets. Of course corporate strategists and marketing departments adjust the organization's long-range positioning (in capabilities and products) to address needs created by these trends. But forward-looking sales departments also study how they can tap into changing consumer attitudes caused by such mega trends.

A maker of heating and air-conditioning equipment, for example, realized that perceptions about climate change and sensitivity to energy prices already have a real impact on when and why consumers decide to buy new equipment. The company has developed a model that incorporates different scenarios for energy prices and other key drivers of energy demand. Each scenario includes implications for different types of customers, including likely demand for each client and which products to highlight.

For example, in a scenario with steeply increasing oil prices, more customers are expected to purchase heating systems based on alternative fuels or add modules to use solar energy. Those interdependencies have been modeled based on market and customer data. The results are translated into sales targets for different product groups and insights to guide sales force tactics and define incentives. The model is frequently updated to ensure it incorporates fresh data and thinking. There are also periodic "reality checks" to make sure that the program still reflects likely scenarios. This process allows the company to turn a very broad trend into practical insights for the sales team and gives it a leg up in a competitive marketplace.

Invest ahead of demand

Forward-looking sales programs also depend on access to resources: companies have to be willing to take risks now to get themselves out ahead, creating sales capacity long before the revenue will materialize.

Many executives explicitly account for investment in new growth opportunities in their annual capacity planning processes.

Many sales executives we interviewed explicitly account for investment in new growth opportunities in their annual capacity planning processes. While this usually involves simply drawing territories and assigning customer lists to support growth initiatives, it can also include requests for dedicated resources to pursue new sources of long-term demand, particularly in emerging markets. The level of investment can be as high as 2 to 3 percent of selling costs—small in percentage terms but a significant commitment in an environment where sales leaders fight for each dollar of investment.

The ability to commit in advance helped one Asian auto company crack the Indian market. As it assessed India in the late 1990s, the prospects for success for foreign manufacturers were not clear-cut. There was little doubt that the nation's rapidly expanding middle class would boost demand for cars, but tapping into that growth from the outside was not going to be simple. A big constraint was developing the right distribution network since many of the best dealers were already tied to existing local manufacturers.

The conventional approach would be to piggyback on a local manufacturer's network and partner with dealers in the largest cities first to gain presence quickly. This is the least expensive and fastest way to attack a new region. However, it had limited upside for the carmaker. The leading dealers tended to put their domestic brands first and only dealers in the big cities could afford to support a second brand. Without real focus from dealers, the prospects of becoming market leader were far from certain.

This knowledge prompted the company to look further into the future. Although economic growth was concentrated in the largest cities now, it was undoubtedly spreading and a new wave of middle-class Indians would arise in second- and third-tier cities in just a few years. A player that had a dealer network in place in those cities before demand materialized would be exceptionally well positioned.

The sales leadership laid out a plan to sign up more than 110 dedicated dealers across India, including in secondary cities. The plan involved recruiting two specific types of dealers—small independents and sellers of minor brands who were eager to expand. The company focused heavily on each dealer's personal aspiration to grow and his or her willingness to buy into a five-year vision. Beyond the largest cities, dealers would need to stay lean in the early years when demand would be low. This meant the owner would have to be flexible, operating with a small staff that would have to double up in management roles. In many cases, the owner would also have to act as new- and used-car manager. Then, when demand started to grow, the dealers would need to scale up and invest. Recruiting dealers who fit this profile would be a sales project in itself.

The first challenge, however, was building the conviction to bankroll this unorthodox approach. Complicating matters, the company had just one product suitable for the Indian market— others were in the pipeline but as much as two years away. However, the sales executive believed that this distribution strategy would capture the full potential of the Indian market because the dealers would be fully focused on his brand and the automaker would have an important first-mover advantage in smaller cities.

The company also decided to offer subsidies to help the dealers through the early years, arguing that the eventual sales volume and associated profits justified this upfront investment. The subsidy would come in the form of incentives to help the dealer pay for its facilities and build new vehicle and parts inventory— expensive capital outlays required to add a new brand. The incentives were calibrated to enable the dealer to break even in the early, lean years.

Once the plan was approved, the second challenge was convincing more than 50 dealers to sign up with a foreign franchise. Although the targeted dealers didn't have access to the top domestic brands, they were being courted by other car companies trying to enter India. What sealed the deal for many was the announcement that the Asian automaker would build a local production facility. This was an important differentiator, reinforcing the manufacturer's long-term commitment to the market.

The results have been extraordinary and fully justified the sales team's vision. Within two years, the company introduced additional models and gained enough volume to withdraw the dealer subsidies and attract additional dealers. Within five years, the original network had doubled and the company was in the top five for market share in India

> An above-average return on sales of 8 percent meant the company had exceeded its initial sales investment many times over.

and it enjoyed top-tier customer satisfaction. An above-average return on sales of 8 percent meant the company had exceeded its initial sales investment many times over.

Make it a way of life

Such success stories are of little relevance if they are just a stroke of luck and can't be replicated. From what we learned in our interviews, they are not. Sales executives make their own luck by developing the ability to peek around corners and consistently identify sales opportunities that may not materialize for 12 or 18 months—or longer.

How do these managers decide when to pounce on a tactical opportunity or commit in advance to investments in a market that will pay off years from now? The leaders we interviewed do not simply gamble on market movements—they have

> Leaders do not simply gamble on market movements—they have institutionalized a forward-looking approach.

institutionalized a forward-looking approach. They do their homework and have a fact-based rationale for new initiatives and investments. And they have built a track record of success that gives them credibility in their organizations.

There are many ways of generating this forward-looking view of the market. As we mentioned earlier, one IT company has created a high-powered solutions unit that is dedicated to preparing major customers to commit early to new trends. The team is staffed with a mix of former consultants, professors, and respected industry leaders from high-potential market segments. Its task is to find ways to accelerate demand by influencing important decision makers to be early adopters.

The ultimate goal is to help the company get customers to commit to investing in the next evolution of technology ahead of its competitors. So, the group spends its time producing thought-provoking industry perspectives, quantifying the benefits of its offering for individual companies, and building relationships with influential company executives and government officials. If its ideas are compelling it can reduce adoption time for new technology and accelerate uptake in an entire customer segment or country. If it succeeds, its company benefits disproportionately, given its existing share and position.

A contract manufacturing company that builds products for IT equipment makers has had great success with a dedicated "trends analysis" function. It deploys a team of speculative market analysts whose job is to predict which hardware products will have meaningful volume in the next two to three years—and which potential client companies are likely to develop such products. That gives the company a perspective on its target customers a couple of years before they become large.

The contract manufacturer uses several strategies to build these insights, including spending time with the venture capital firms that fund new companies, talking to customers about which emerging products and technologies they are pursuing, and continuously evaluating the supply chains of its customers (and of its customers' customers) for emerging sales targets.

One of the outputs of this analysis is a list of small but fast-growing companies that may evolve into major users of contract manufacturing capacity. The manufacturer then invests in building relationships with these companies to convert them into customers. The investment is essentially a subsidy—taking on a customer whose initial volume is too low to be economically attractive. Some of these emerging companies will never grow into marquee customers. A few, however, will become major players, and the manufacturer will have locked in a profitable order stream. In less than two years, this group was consistently able to deliver a 15 percent return on its investment by identifying new opportunities the company would have otherwise been unlikely to get.

Building and sustaining the capability to take a forward-looking view of the market is not easy. As we looked across all of these great sellers, two common characteristics emerged: the mindset of sales leadership and resource commitment. Sales leaders must consistently monitor the macro-environment in search of sales opportunities. Even good sales leaders find this challenging, given the relentless pressure to hit near-term targets. This is why resource commitment is important.

> Forward planning must be part of someone's job description—not just part of top management's lengthy to-do list.

In other words, forward planning must be part of someone's job description—not just part of top management's lengthy to-do list. Sometimes it falls within marketing but, in many cases, it is sales' responsibility. The level of investment will vary, depending on the company and its context. At the high end, we see formal operations such as the market-shaping team at the IT supplier. At the other end, forward-looking analysis is embedded into annual capacity planning. The most common arrangement is a small centralized sales team whose responsibility is to scan opportunities and convert those it finds into tangible sales opportunities. Many companies we see investing real resources ahead of demand are equally rigorous in taking costs out of sales. A conscious eye to where resources are no longer important creates the capacity to invest.

Thinking three moves ahead is a vital tactic in any game and is essential to sales growth. It does not come automatically, however. It requires companies to recognize the value of monitoring and interpreting external trends. It requires budgets that take into account the long lead times for exploiting emerging sales opportunities. Finally, it requires sales leaders who can drive results today, while building the insights and ideas to score first in tomorrow's game.

In the next chapter, we'll see how top sales managers don't just take this macro-view of opportunities; they're also able to turn the microscope onto their existing markets to find the untapped pockets of growth.

William J. Teuber, Jr.
Vice-Chairman, EMC

How do you anticipate mega trends such as cloud computing?

We use a multipronged approach. We follow our cutting-edge customers closely to see what they are doing. We listen to our engineers—our innovation engine—to hear where they want to drive things. We have a sophisticated business development team that monitors new company formation carefully. We work with research universities to discover which emerging technologies have potential commercial applications. Then we marry all of that thinking with what our customers are thinking. Trends don't appear clearly from any one source. They come into focus when you bring a mixture of perspectives together.

How has your go-to-market model scaled up with your dramatic growth?

It has scaled with our opportunity. We have learned to focus where our opportunity exists, both with current customers and outside our base. We identify opportunities by region and by customer, and we get very granular with irrefutable data to see where we can move the needle. Having that discipline gives us the ability to devise a plan to capture dramatic growth through our direct sales force as well as through channel partners.

How do you reconcile the quarterly heartbeat of your sales organization with the need to invest ahead of demand to capture long-term opportunities?

In a publicly-traded company with a public report card every 90 days, you have to do both. In our international operations, we introduced a three-year sales planning process to get beyond the 90-day mentality of "How will I make my number this quarter?". We monitor how markets are going to develop and prioritize opportunities that will generate the best growth over the next four to eight quarters. We've also created a Rapid Growth Markets Board made up of senior leaders who hold meetings in those markets and link back to the rest of the company, so people in product development can plan accordingly.

You have almost doubled revenues in the past five years, and are planning to grow faster than your markets. How do you sustain such growth?

You have to have the right strategy and the right offering, and your sales organization has to communicate the benefits of that to the customer. In order to build our portfolio and market reach, we've bought 35 companies over the last five years. Doing cross-company sales integration successfully is one of the hardest things to do. We've learned a lot from experience.

Ultimately, you have to have the best people to execute your strategy. I'm betting my job on everyone who works for me. Therefore, I'm going to select the top people to represent our company in the marketplace. EMC has what I consider to be the gold standard of sales forces. There is an aura about it. To be in sales at EMC is a badge of honor. That's why we attract and retain the right people—to make sure we have the best talent bench in our sales force.

2. Mine growth beneath the surface

"We shall not cease from exploration, and the end of all our exploring will be to arrive where we started and know the place for the first time."

—T.S. Eliot

The old cliché is that you can't tell the forest for the trees. In finding new sources of sales growth, the more relevant analogy is the reverse: by looking at the forest of average data it's easy to miss where growth truly lies. For example, it is widely known that US manufacturing is in a state of decline. In 2008 alone, manufacturing GDP fell by $44 billion. But if you disaggregate that number, you will find that there were healthy pockets of growth that amounted to almost $32 billion—four times India's total growth that year.[4] The hidden pockets of growth in your industry may lay in your own backyard.

---

4   US Bureau of Economics; Moody's economy.com

In the previous chapter, we showed how sales leaders can get ahead of competitors by capturing growth based on trends and investing ahead of demand. This chapter takes a look at sales executives who unearthed growth by undertaking micro-market analysis, identifying which markets have the highest growth potential, and aligning their resources to capture them.

> Although the company had 20 percent of the overall market, in some of the fastest-growing segments, its share was as low as 10 percent.

A global chemicals and services provider increased the growth rate of new accounts from 15 to 25 percent in just one year. The big breakthrough, a sales executive told us, was adopting a more granular view of the market. Instead of looking at current sales by region, as it had always done, the company developed a new and far more revealing view by examining share within customer industry sectors within specific US counties. This deeper level of analysis revealed that although the company had 20 percent of the overall market, it had up to 60 percent in some micro-markets, while in others, including some of the fastest-growing segments, its share was as low as 10 percent.

Sales leaders used this insight to turn the planning process on its head. Instead of relying solely on historical data to allocate resources, they included forward-looking opportunity data at a much finer level of analysis. They adjusted how the sales force was deployed to exploit the growth opportunities and ensured that reps were equipped to win in the opportunity hot spots they had discovered.

The sales leaders we interviewed across a range of sectors agreed that taking this sort of granular approach to growth is essential in deciding where to compete and in translating market insights into actions. The most successful sales leaders were extremely proactive in mining the growth that lay right beneath their feet in what seemed to be mature markets. Many have delivered impressive results thanks to this micro-market approach to growth, even under the strain of the financial crisis. At the core of this approach to find growth ahead of competition, leading sales organizations do three things:

- **Find the pockets of growth.** Using micro-market analysis, companies can identify where opportunity lies at a very granular level based on a combination of market characteristics, including competitive intensity, and market attractiveness.

- **Look beyond sales to mine growth.** To maximize the benefits of micro-markets, leading organizations recognize they need to involve functions beyond sales.

- **Keep it easy for the sales team.** Micro-market strategies by their very nature are heavy on the analytics, so it's important that sales teams on the ground don't get bogged down by the detail and can simply harness the information in the most effective way.

Find the pockets of growth

Granularity is a word traditionally used more by scientists than sales leaders, yet it cropped up time and again in our conversations. Companies that have capitalized on micro-markets have taken a geological hammer to all their market and customer data; they break larger markets down into much smaller units, where the opportunities—prospects, new customer segments, or micro-segments—can be assessed in detail.

> It quickly becomes clear that a broad-brush approach will not lead you to the most lucrative hot spots.

Take the healthcare industry in the US, for example. Many industry experts expect the US market to go into hyper growth between 2010 and 2014, after implementation of the Patient Protection and Affordable Care Act. However, growth will not be uniform across the country. Under one scenario, the market for individual health policies will approximately triple by 2014. Yet, growth rates will vary by a factor of seven between states and by a factor of 20 at the county level (Exhibit 3). It quickly becomes clear that a broad-brush approach will not lead you to the most lucrative hot spots and could leave you wasting resources where growth is significantly below average. Leading healthcare companies are taking differentiated approaches to driving revenue growth based on this type of granular information. For example, some retail healthcare companies are using the data to guide store location decisions: counties that might be unattractive today due to the high uninsured population will actually turn into high-growth markets after the healthcare reform is fully implemented.

In Europe, a consumer telecommunications company reexamined its 15 sales regions and split them into approximately 500 micro-markets based on a variety of characteristics such as shopper population density and store catchment areas. Sales leaders were surprised to see that

EXHIBIT 3

Micro-market analysis reveals pockets of growth

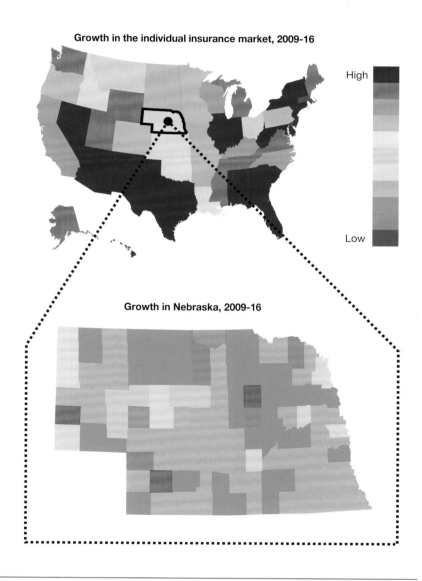

Growth in the individual insurance market, 2009-16

High

Low

Growth in Nebraska, 2009-16

when viewed at this level of detail, these markets actually varied by a factor of four in terms of shopping activity, economic growth, and wealth. Focusing the microscope on its store penetration in each micro-market and looking at the relative share of stores compared to competitors showed similarly wide variations.

It became apparent that there were deep pockets of opportunity in places with attractive populations and limited competition, but the company did not have the right store footprint or formats to access this untapped demand. There were also places where competition was intense but there were fewer unserved customers than the telecommunications company had initially believed. It had treated many of these markets in similar ways due to the lack of granular, micro-level segmentation. The head of channels realized quickly that it was time for a much more differentiated approach if the company was to grow revenue profitably.

> The company shaved total store costs by 5 percent by eliminating, resizing, or refocusing less profitable locations.

The company aggregated its 500 micro-markets into four categories. In the most underserved markets with the lowest density of retail stores (both its own and those of competitors) the company focused on developing different store formats to make store economics more attractive and establish a foothold before its competitors. Ultimately, the telecommunications company saw 5 to 10 percent more in-store visits by optimizing its store footprint. It also shaved total store costs by 5 percent by eliminating, resizing, or refocusing less profitable locations.

EXHIBIT 4

Micro-market lens fills the pipeline with otherwise hidden opportunities

Industry opportunities, percentage

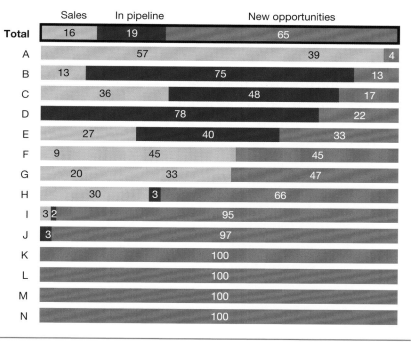

	Sales	In pipeline	New opportunities
Total	16	19	65
A		57	39 · 4
B	13	75	13
C	36	48	17
D		78	22
E	27	40	33
F	9	45	45
G	20	33	47
H	30	3	66
I	3·2		95
J	3		97
K			100
L			100
M			100
N			100

The chemicals and services company we mentioned at the start of the chapter created a group of prospectors who sifted through data from external resources and analyzed information gathered by the field sales force. The head of sales asked this group to translate the micro-market insights into specific sales leads. The results were impressive: a ten-fold increase in prospects in some micro-markets and a narrowing down of realistic prospects in others. Exhibit 4 shows the scale of the variation.[5] In industries I to N, for example, it calculated that there was an enormous missing opportunity, whereas industries A to D, for example, were already close to their full potential.

---

5   Company analysis.

Look beyond sales

Translating detailed analysis into insights is not a novel idea in itself. Nor is it sufficient for capturing micro-market growth ahead of competition. What turns insights into sales is how the front line is managed in the micro-market. The sales executives we interviewed stressed the need for appropriate resource allocation and actionable tactics for sales teams or retail stores to fully exploit the new opportunities.

> Not all resource allocation decisions are at the discretion of the head of sales, so cross-functional collaboration is critical to extract the full value of the micro-market pockets of growth.

These sales executives also work very closely with other parts of the organization to capture the most lucrative customer opportunities in micro-markets. This means realigning sales, marketing, and sometimes even noncommercial resources such as customer services or supply chain. Of course, not all resource allocation decisions are at the discretion of the head of sales, so cross-functional collaboration is critical to extract the full value of the micro-market pockets of growth.

Marketing plays a substantial role both in generating micro-market insights and in applying them in the field. For example, an Asian telecommunications company discovered that about 20 percent of its marketing budget was being spent in markets with the lowest lifetime customer value. The company reallocated its marketing dollars to the most lucrative half of its markets, which represented more than two-thirds of its opportunity, and saw a 10 percent improvement in revenue in those markets in one year.

EXHIBIT 5

Redesigned territories better match rep time with opportunity

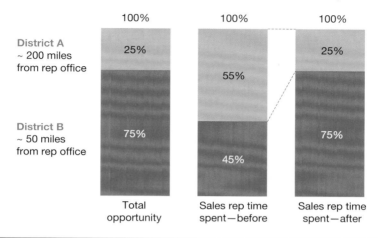

The executives we talked to believe that assigning resources from their own sales organization based on previous demand patterns is quite literally yesterday's game. At the chemicals and services company, one sales rep spent more than half her time 200 miles from her home office, even though only a quarter of her region's opportunity sat there. This was purely because sales territories had been assigned according to historical performance rather than on growth prospects. After going through the micro-market analysis, the company realized the mismatch. Now, the rep spends 75 percent of her time in an area where 75 percent of the opportunity exists—within 50 miles of her office (Exhibit 5).

Some companies have used nontraditional sales techniques to exploit new micro-segments. One European integrated telecommunications provider saw a 35 percent increase in call center revenue after just six weeks of actively turning inbound service calls into sales. By analyzing customer data at a very detailed level and developing tailored value propositions its customer service agents were able to make extremely targeted pitches when customers rang up for general service support (although sales were not attempted if the customer was complaining). Companies from the US and Canada have seen similar results.

Keep it easy for the sales team

Sales teams have neither the time nor inclination to delve into the data or worry about cross-functional resource allocation. If the micro-market approach is to work, complexity has to be minimized and the sales team needs simple and effective insights and tools.

> If the micro-market approach is to work, complexity has to be minimized.

A North American logistics company had an overall goal to increase prices by 3 percent annually, but it knew that wide variation in growth and competitive intensity across its markets might make this difficult to pull off. To ensure it met this target, it developed a detailed micro-market pricing scheme and provided simple rules, based on the competitive dynamics of each segment: reps in high-growth markets were expected to raise prices and grow faster and those in declining markets were allowed to reduce prices to prevent existing customers from leaving.

This new, simple approach worked well. In prior years, sales teams had always been in the dark as to how prices were set. Now, they could easily understand what was driving the differences. The new approach also made performance management easier as reps could now accept that local market characteristics were being taken into account and they could be benchmarked against peers from similar markets.

A cargo airline developed a complex micro-market strategy to categorize customers based on flight/space availability and demand. While the airline realized that demand varied by time of day, day of the week (for example, shipping fresh sea bass from Italy on a Wednesday for weekend consumption in New York), and week of the year, (for example, shipping flowers the week before Valentine's Day), it lacked a systematic way to capture the information to inform daily decisions regarding key accounts such as how much capacity to allocate to each customer. The airline's new customer categorization model essentially evaluated the "balance of trade" with its customers, recognizing which customers were contributing more to challenging micro-markets and rewarding them accordingly.

The impact of this analysis was tremendous because it helped the company identify opportunities for different negotiation strategies, including providing space on flights on routes with high demand while also raising prices, and asking for higher volume commitments for flights on lower-demand routes. Given the dynamics of the cargo market, which is very susceptible to changes in flight itineraries and shifts in customers' own supply chains, this became a very complex model.

To make it easy for the sales force, the company developed a simple performance dashboard for sales teams to manage pricing and volume negotiations with large customers, by route on a daily basis. The dashboard includes critical information, such as whether the specific flight is overbooked or not, as well as

A simple performance dashboard allowed sales teams to manage pricing and volume negotiations with large customers.

information on the weekly itineraries of the airline and its competitors. The sales manager holds weekly sales strategy discussions with each rep to ensure they are always well placed to achieve the desired outcomes. This effort generated a share of wallet as high as 20 percent with key customers.

Micro-market strategies give sales leaders a powerful way to find growth ahead of their competitors. The sales leaders we met have expanded their analytical capabilities to find those micro-pockets of growth, they have gone beyond sales to reallocate their company-wide resources against those opportunities, and they have made it easy for their sales reps to pursue pockets of growth in a profitable way.

Alejandro Munoz
Vice-President, Americas and
Global Production, DuPont Pioneer

How do you find hot spots of growth?

We started using the micro-market approach a few years
ago in North America. We started to add external data
on competitive intelligence and market research as well
as feedback from the field teams to our overall sales and
marketing data. The effect was amazing. We went from
using North American averages to granular insights that
we would never have seen otherwise. This micro-level of
understanding of the size and nature of the opportunity
meant we could manage our geography in a much
more differentiated way. We evolved from a monolithic
North American structure to initially four and then seven
business units that have a lot of autonomy. We also
increased our sales areas from 20 to more than 40 to
allow for a more differentiated way of managing
the field.

What has been the impact of the new approach?

We have been able to increase our market share in recent
years, following 13 consecutive years of market share loss
before the micro-market approach. Over the past three to
four years, we've won back share in our two core product
lines, more than 5 percentage points of share in corn and
more than 10 points in soy beans.

How do you align your resources to these hot spots?

Once we have a handle on the opportunities at the micro-market level, we prioritize them and invest accordingly. This means each area takes a different medicine. The big change from the past is that from having averages that hid market realities we can now respond much better. Overall, we increased our number of customer-facing resources by a third.

How do you embed the micro-market approach in your company?

You have to commit to it. This granular view is really a new way of thinking. If you are not ready to deal with the complexity, then don't even start. You need a clear understanding of the level of detail you can cope with. If you get too detailed, you get tangled up in the weeds. Our approach differs by market; the concepts are the same, but the details vary. For example, the northeast has a lot of small dairy farms, and the opportunity there is as different from that in the US corn belt as the North American opportunity in total differs from that in China.

How do you make this approach easy for every sales rep?

You need to end up with a very short list of what you ask reps to contribute in terms of data so you don't eat into their time. In terms of rolling out the different approaches, we make sure we have a clear, consistent message. And we've found you have to repeat it many different times and in many different settings. Keep it easy so people can get their heads around it, and it takes time for it to become part of the company's DNA. In our case, it took some years to move from it being an interesting concept to one that guided how we run our commercial operations, how we invest against opportunities, and how we deploy sales and marketing tactics against those opportunities.

Part two:
Sell the way your customers want

"What do my customers want from the sales experience?" Our leading sales executives ask themselves this question almost daily. Sadly, not all companies do this. Many pour millions from their marketing budgets into researching what customers want from their products, but our research shows that sales experience can be as important.

Knowing what customers do and don't want from the sales experience is imperative. Finding out, however, is not straightforward. Asking customers about their preferences does not generate the real insights needed to craft a compelling sales experience. What customers say does not always match what customers do. Across both business and consumer markets, customers tend to say that price is more important and sales experience less important. The way they act suggests otherwise.

McKinsey proprietary research highlighted the importance of the sales experience and the challenge of relying only on what customers say. We asked 1,200 B2B purchasers what drove their purchasing decision, and "overall sales experience" came out as the least important category (Exhibit 6).[6] We then asked the same customers to rate their suppliers' performance and also asked for each supplier's share of that customer's business. Correlating supplier performance with actual purchases revealed a startlingly different picture. Sales experience was three times

---

6   McKinsey & Company survey.

EXHIBIT 6

Sales experience is more important than customers tell you

Survey of 1,200 B2B purchasers; percentage

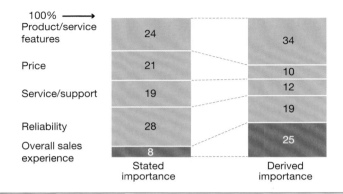

more important than stated. This gives a more accurate picture of the sales experience's role in driving purchases.

Those sales executives who understand the importance of sales experience also have to know what customers do and don't want from that experience. What they really don't want is too much contact unless a vendor has something valuable to say; customers want more from a sales interaction than just a cozy chat. The great sellers we'll meet in the next few chapters have designed their sales models with this firmly in mind.

Sales experience also plays a major role in consumer purchasing decisions. Another McKinsey proprietary survey on the B2C sales experience shows that customer satisfaction drives customer lifetime value in several ways and certainly creates a positive ROI. Once companies achieve the breakthrough to outstanding customer satisfaction, positive word-of-mouth recommendations skyrocket and customers actively upgrade service plans, while cancellation rates, churn levels, and service downgrades plummet.

Consumer satisfaction is fragile though. It only takes one or two bad experiences to become very dissatisfied, but it may require many positive interactions to get a "very satisfied" score. In today's digital environment bad news travels even faster. What used to be a lone detracting voice chatting at the water cooler can be quickly amplified

> It only takes one or two bad experiences for a consumer to become very dissatisfied, but it may require many positive interactions to get a "very satisfied" score.

via a social media site or online review. Suddenly, one bad sales interaction with an influential person can become a minor catastrophe.

So, sales experience is a major driver of sales. Our interviews revealed many examples of how leading sales executives get this right and improve customer experience across channels through a multichannel selling model. We will showcase some of these practices in the next three chapters:

Chapter 3: Master multichannel sales highlights how great sellers set up a range of channels to serve their customers and how they orchestrate so many channels cost-effectively.

Chapter 4: Innovate direct sales looks at the astonishing impact that optimizing face-to-face and other direct channels can have.

Chapter 5: Invest in partners for mutual profit talks about going beyond vendors' own resources and collaborating with indirect channel partners to everyone's benefit.

3. Master multichannel sales

"The real art of conducting consists in transitions."

— *Gustav Mahler*

During the height of the dot.com boom, many industry analysts predicted that the Internet would soon dominate automotive retailing, at the expense of traditional dealers. More than a decade later, their forecasts have turned out to be only half right. Dealers are still the primary channel for cars sold around the world, but the Internet is undeniably important. Rather than talking to a dealer, customers are increasingly turning to the Internet for advice.

The idea of multiple sales channels is not new, but few companies have truly mastered their multichannel capability, falling victim to channel conflict or overspending. One automotive company has risen to this challenge. It realized that customers were getting a very inconsistent brand experience given the difference between its own website and dealers' Internet sites. The response was an integrated multichannel strategy. It invested heavily in a multilocal website approach that referred all customers to the website of the shopper's nearest dealer. The dealers' websites then not only had a common look and feel in order to represent the brand consistently, but also featured the company's most relevant product, option, and service content. The automotive company even played down its national brand website in favor of its dealers' sites.

So that's two channels accounted for. But it didn't stop there. Sales leaders then tied in the other channels that touched customers: the call center worked closely with dealers to make sure that customer concerns were addressed; the captive finance division coordinated with the dealers at the end of a lease, passing on the lead and ensuring that the dealer had the best chance to retain the customer.

By knitting together all of these different direct and indirect channels, the company was able to deliver a consistently positive customer experience in every channel. That experience helped push its flagship brand to a leading position in its core markets.

As this automaker's experience shows, channels continue to proliferate and morph—from dealers to catalogs to online to social networking sites. And customer preferences continue to evolve—and can change from day to day. Leading sellers use insights into these shifting customer behaviors to create opportunities to update their channel mix and differentiate themselves. They quickly adjust their go-to-market routes and—with equal speed—scale back investments in other channels to manage overall costs.

At a basic level, multichannel management seems straightforward—assigning customers to channels by value: low-cost channels, such as online and telesales, for smaller customers and high-cost channels, such as face-to-face sales, for key accounts. But this is a simplistic approach that overlooks how buyers really behave. The same major account that demands white-glove service from your direct sales force may not want to see your rep for every little

> The same major account that demands white-glove service from your direct sales force may not want to see your rep for every little transaction.

transaction. Sometimes, it wants to interact online or talk to a product expert on the phone. Also, some products start out in one channel and then migrate to others. The successful multichannel leaders we talked to emphasized flexibility—help customers shift between channels if they wish, to provide the experience they want.

The effort is worthwhile: mastering multichannel sales pays off. Companies that get it right generally enjoy larger profit margins and revenue growth. For example, in banking, product penetration and revenue per client can be about twice higher when customers are served across more than four channels, compared to customers that are served only through one channel (Exhibit 7).[7]

In this chapter, we will look at four aspects of multichannel management and show how leading companies have tackled them:

- **Blend remote sales and field sales.** Many companies have adopted remote sales as a low-cost way to serve smaller customers. Leading sellers have innovated by blending their remote sales with their traditional sales forces to drive growth while lowering costs.

---

7   McKinsey & Company multichannel survey.

EXHIBIT 7
Banking customers who use more channels spend more

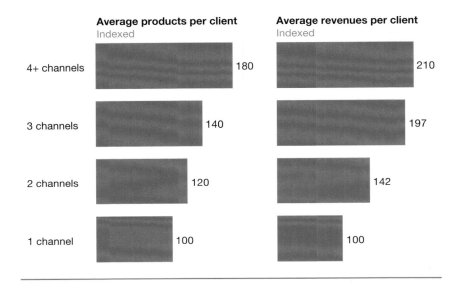

Average products per client
Indexed

Average revenues per client
Indexed

	Average products per client	Average revenues per client
4+ channels	180	210
3 channels	140	197
2 channels	120	142
1 channel	100	100

- **Integrate online and offline.** A digital sales strategy has become imperative for many companies. The sales leaders we talked to have integrated their online and digital channels with other sales channels, seamlessly serving customers across online and offline channels.

- **Orchestrate direct and indirect channels.** For leading sellers, going direct or indirect is no longer a binary choice. They build selling approaches that take advantage of their capabilities and those of their channel partners.

- **Bring service channels into the fold.** Good companies understand that great service drives tomorrow's growth. The leading executives we interviewed have demonstrated that great service can drive today's growth as well. They effectively use each service interaction with customers as an occasion to sell.

Blend remote sales and field sales

Even the most gilt-edged customers neither want nor need a sales rep coming around to complete an order that they could easily place themselves over the phone. It may be better for both parties to have well-trained telesales reps maintain accounts and drive penetration—an approach that both lowers service costs and improves customer satisfaction.

At a high-tech hardware provider, sales teams sold equipment to large enterprises, typically with a three-year contract. Reps were assigned many accounts in their territories to ensure they had enough customers to make their targets. However, the company was missing out on smaller transactions because reps could not afford to spend time with customers who were still two years away from renewing their contracts.

> Collaboration between inside and field sales increased sales force productivity by 14 percent and margins by up to 20 percent.

The sales managers decided to create an enterprise sales team that paired each field sales rep with a phone sales rep. The phone rep kept in constant touch with clients during the off-contract, managed the sales of accessories and smaller transactions, and alerted field sales reps to any large deals or opportunities that might arise. This collaborative approach increased sales force productivity by 14 percent. The program also included a clever upselling scheme. Phone reps were given incentives to push higher-margin solutions and used their influence with the field reps and customers to promote them. In some regions, this led to margin improvements of up to 20 percent higher than those where only field reps specified configurations.

Some companies blur the lines even more between remote sales and field sales. A software company has created phone sales hubs to serve small and mid-size customers. Those reps spend 80 percent of their time on the phone selling but take two trips a month to the field to close larger deals. It is by far the company's most productive sales group.

Align compensation

A major challenge facing any company that wants to master multichannel sales is getting the incentive and compensation model right. The very best sales executives use incentives not just to ensure harmony across channels but also to fine-tune channel performance.

For example, in order to move small customers to lower-cost channels, an industrial company pays field reps commissions for all customer revenue, regardless of channel.

A global telecommunications player incentivizes reps to hand off accounts that are becoming more complex to the next higher tier—moving an account from a phone rep to a field rep, for example.

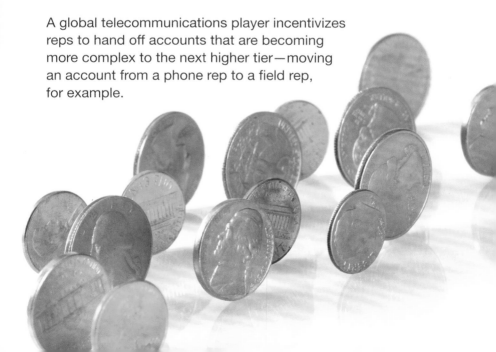

Integrate online and offline

Nowhere is the world of multichannel selling more dynamic than in consumer products. And perhaps nowhere is the opportunity greater. Recent McKinsey research shows that consumers who shop across a number of channels—physical stores, online, catalogs—spend about four times more annually than those who shop in just one. The challenge facing sales executives today is to create easy routes to accommodate consumers as they move between online and offline channels.

Consider the multichannel strategies of two major retailers: Swedish home products group IKEA and US department store chain JCPenney. IKEA uses its Web channel primarily to support its stores. It does not even offer online sales in many countries. Instead, its website primarily provides information that reinforces the company's reputation for innovative products and low prices, as well as real-time information on store inventory and shelf locations

Retailers that have used multichannel strategies to fuel sustainable growth tightly integrate their strategies across all online and offline channels.

that helps customers plan their store visits. By contrast, JCPenney has built on its legacy as a successful catalog merchant to deliver a tightly integrated cross-channel offering. Stores are outfitted with Web kiosks, and all point-of-sale terminals have Web access so customers can easily order products that are not in stock. The company is even testing a system that allows customers to scan coupons in the store that have been sent directly to their mobile telephones.

Retailers that have used multichannel strategies to fuel sustainable growth tightly integrate their strategies across all online and offline channels. Each channel plays a clear (and often quite distinct) role in supporting and reinforcing the overall brand experience.

Orchestrate direct and indirect channels

Companies can find it hard to hand valuable customers over to indirect channel partners such as resellers. However, they also recognize that a direct model is not always appropriate for all accounts. We address indirect channels in much more detail in chapter 5, but here we're interested in how leading sales organizations get their direct and indirect channels to play harmoniously.

> Countries where the new model was tested achieved a 50 percent higher growth rate.

The head of sales at a high-tech industry leader decided to mix direct and indirect resources, taking into account partners' capabilities in specific market segments. The handful of European countries where this was tested achieved a growth rate 50 percent higher than the countries without this model. Analyzing coverage revealed that a lot of in-house direct sales reps were working medium-level accounts, and the company wasn't making the most of partners' reach. Some partners tended to lack sufficient technical skills, while direct reps did not always have time to cover their wide territories. This sales executive decided to adopt two simple ideas.

The first was to get partners more involved in mid-range segments, using in-house sales support to help close deals and to provide technical resources. He allocated phone-based sales reps and technical experts to work with partners, creating a direct-indirect model whereby in-house sales reps generated leads, which they passed onto partners to close.

The second idea was to move from a system in which a rep's territory was based on a quota of closed deals to one in which the quota was for each of the partners he or she would manage and support. With this model, the sales executive could ensure reps would not pursue deals themselves but would instead spend all their time with partners, and help them close deals.

Channel choices can also change according to product life cycles. A high-tech company uses a hybrid model: when a product is new, it is sold by the direct sales force. Later in the life cycle, when adoption is high—and there is more competitive pressure— the product is handed off to partners.

Bring service channels into the fold

Many leading sales organizations turn to channels outside of the sales function to supplement sales or to provide leads. Integrating these new channels into sales might seem like an unnecessary headache, but the sales executives we spoke to saw it very differently.

Customer service teams, for example, often have intimate knowledge of customers, are in frequent contact with them, and can be in a position of trust when they are helpful. It's the perfect relationship on which to build sales.

A large European cable provider ramped up sales through its service department. It had more than a thousand service agents across five call centers, but they weren't helping push revenue by getting existing customers to add "sticky" products, such as premium TV packages. When managers investigated, they found that the service agents did not believe sales could be a part of the service relationship and some were uncomfortable proposing new solutions.

The initial focus of sales leaders therefore was to instill conviction and confidence about selling among service reps. There was no change to service staff's incentive structure, rather managers explained that part of helping customers was making sure that they had the products and services that best met their needs. Managers coached the call center agents to think differently, from providing customer services to providing customer services and responding to other needs the customer may have (Exhibit 8). This initiative quickly increased conversion rates from less than 1 percent to 5 to 6 percent of calls and annual new sales revenue by 15 percent.

> The initial focus of sales leaders was to instill conviction and confidence about selling among service reps.

A global industrial company also uses customer service reps to generate sales but, more unusually, it also turned to its drivers to boost revenue, finding a way to integrate this delivery channel into the sales function. When drivers visit customers and see competitors' activities, they hand out promotional leaflets that refer back to the company's website. They also pass the information back to sales staff via their handheld computers. These customers' future activity can then be tracked, allowing the company to reward drivers who generate qualified leads or closed sales (rather than simply based on volume of referrals). This driver referral program more than doubled revenue from the company's overall employee-driven lead generation program.

EXHIBIT 8
Using services as a sales channel

From a service mindset ...		**... to a "service and sales" mindset**

From a service mindset ...

"We must provide better service before we earn the right to sell."

... to a "service and sales" mindset

"I understand my customers' needs and they appreciate my advice."

"My customers are busy. I serve them best by efficiently processing their requests."

"I love solving my customers' problems and showing them how they can better use our products and services."

"I am not serving my customers well if I talk them into something."

"I couldn't sleep if I didn't follow up."

Understanding how to integrate these nonsales functions into the channel mix is the hallmark of successful sales organizations and captures perfectly the essence of mastering the complex challenges of multichannel management.

It is important for companies to review their routes to market regularly and to manage them actively. To manage the complexity of multiple channels, some of the sales leaders we spoke to hold country-wide weekly multichannel management meetings. These allow managers to rebalance marketing budgets and channel strategies. One high-tech provider lets regional general managers choose how customers are allocated to its four channels based on local nuances.

A core lesson from our interviews is that a great deal of growth and profit goes unrealized because multichannel opportunities are not properly captured. No matter what approach you take to managing multiple channels, it is critical to build an economic understanding of ROI by channel. Many companies do this by understanding the value of growth options and ranking them by their potential returns and relative difficulty. Systematically analyzing different options enables companies to make trade-offs such as deciding whether to invest in mobile commerce or aim for driving higher in-store sales.

Of course excellent multichannel management is of little consequence if individual channels are not optimized. In the next two chapters we look at direct sales and then partners to see how world-class sales organizations extract the most value from these channels.

Gregory Lee
President and CEO, Asia, Samsung

What is your approach to multichannel sales?

Our approach is to build depth of expertise, processes, and relationships with multiple channels and take advantage of our product portfolio, innovation, and design synergies across channels. We sell more than 30 product categories to consumers and business customers, and we do so through many channels such as: telecommunications operators, consumer electronics (CE) retailers, specialist electronics retailers, IT resellers, and a direct sales force for our large customers.

Our wide product range and deep channel relationships are an important competitive advantage for us and our channel partners. For example, we initially sold the Samsung Galaxy Tab with phone functionality mainly to telecommunications operators. We then broadened our distribution channels and sold it (with integrated Wi-Fi) to CE retailers and IT channels. Similarly, we sell TVs and large-format displays to retailers, telecommunications operators, and large commercial complexes (for example, airports, shopping centers, hotels and resorts). We have cross-category product teams who bring the best of Samsung to all our channels; and we have channel teams focused on serving our partners at the varying cost, speed, and complexity of their requirements.

How do you integrate online and retail channels for consumer products?

In our business, the entire consumer purchase cycle and experience is intertwined between online and offine

73

worlds. The vast majority of consumers use digital channels to conduct research prior to their purchase, either by visiting websites or relying on digital word of mouth. Hence, digital channels are critical for driving sales but also for connecting our customers with our brand experience through content and services.

We do not want to compete with our retailers or other channel partners but rather help them replicate our brand experience in their stores or online. We also help them enhance their own value propositions through digital channels. For example, in some markets we help our best channel partners sell selective or exclusive Samsung products with a "shop-to-web" approach which delivers various benefits including reduced storage cost, and also expands their product offering despite their limited shelf space. We help them with in-store displays, and we coach their staff on ways to engage store customers to buy Samsung products at the channel partner's online shop. Lastly, we actively deploy social networks and blogs to monitor and shape digital word of mouth, and engage with consumers.

How do you ensure a consistent customer experience across channels?

In talking about our philosophy to managing our brand experience, we often talk about the notion of "freedom within a global framework." Our approach allows the management of one common set of brand cues and experiences while providing flexibility for product-by-product, market-by-market, and, in some cases, customer-by-customer approaches to brand and consumer experiences. One good example is Samsung.com, which is a common platform for our numerous product lines—both

B2C and B2B—in both advanced and emerging countries. It works under the framework of one brand, one global marketing organization, and one design look and feel. In retail stores, we work with channel partners to ensure they can replicate our brand experience through displays, store formats, and their knowledge of our products.

How do you adapt your multichannel sales approach in emerging markets?

Capturing the phenomenal growth of emerging markets requires a specific approach. We have taken care to adapt our multichannel approach to the unique situations of emerging markets. For example, we have a more active approach to managing distributors. We deploy our own field sales reps in their stores to help them sell our products (which we do very little of in established markets). We have also adapted our sales operations to our retailers' capabilities to have an accurate view of sell-through—data that is much harder to get in emerging markets.

Developing a winning channel approach to emerging markets requires also top management commitment and a strong team of local people. Our senior executive team frequently visits markets in Africa, south-east Asia, and Latin America to gain in-depth understanding of the challenges and to demonstrate our commitment to our channel partners. I personally spend a lot of my time ensuring we have the right leaders in core go-to-market and support functions in our fast and growing emerging markets, from large cities to smaller city branches. Having great local teams and helping them build strong channel partnerships is the foundation for fast growth in emerging markets.

4. Innovate direct sales

"Creativity is thinking up new things. Innovation is doing new things."

— Theodore Levitt

"We need more room in the cabin," said one customer circling a large construction machine. "I agree. I'd also make the windshield bigger," added another. Employees of the heavy equipment company took notes. The visitors continued to walk around the prototype, making more suggestions and more notes.

Sounds like a typical focus group, right? Yes and no. Some of the company employees were from product development, but half were from sales. And the customers were not a randomly-selected cross-section of consumers. These were major fleet buyers, invited to codevelop the products they would be buying. Before the design was finished these customers would get a chance to operate prototypes and see some of their ideas come to life in the final product. Sales executives not only cemented relationships with some of their best customers—who developed a strong commitment to the new model—they helped bring forth a product that cost less to build, yet commanded a 4 percent price premium, and helped grow market share.

This is part of the new face of direct selling. Mastering traditional direct selling models—whether it's in B2B or B2C—is no longer enough for the world's leading sellers. As in the example above, top sellers constantly seek new and creative ways to boost sales and maximize the effectiveness of their organizations. The approaches vary, but the common theme is an overinvestment in the right customers. This chapter delves into how some of the world's top sellers are innovating in their direct channels on three fronts:

- **Engage customers early.** Involving customers long before the actual sale benefits the vendor and the customer alike and can take a variety of forms.

- **Bring your expertise to the table.** Making sure that customers can speak to the right people at the right time is critical in closing sales, yet experts are a scarce resource who must be deployed as effectively as possible.

- **Pursue new prospects relentlessly.** Meaningful sales growth comes only by converting prospects into customers, but this is easier said than done. Traditional hunter/farmer models are not always the best approach. Sales executives we talked to have tuned their prospecting efforts to the big opportunities they see.

Engage customers early

In the introduction to this section of the book, we highlighted the importance of understanding what customers want from the sales experience. As we interviewed leading sales executives, we found that, like the heavy equipment company, they went beyond simply asking customers or analyzing how customers behave to crafting the customer experience. They engaged customers early on in a discussion of how to solve business problems and adapt products and services to provide better solutions. This all leads to sales—eventually—but the focus is on a collaborative problem-solving experience.

The notion shouldn't be confused with the marketing activity of collecting insights in order to better understand customer needs or design better products. This is about sales: creatively extending the sales experience in a way that benefits the customer, drives revenue, and deepens loyalty.

For years, an office products company had understood the merits of engaging with customers before actively selling to them. It had strong products and higher prices than competitors. So its sales department had trouble with standard RFPs, which did not provide a way to convey the advantages of the company's products. This led to price pressure to stay alive in competitive bids.

> Engage customers early on in a discussion of how to adapt products and services to provide better solutions.

Sales leaders at the company had already tried flying in prospective customers to tour the plant and learn about the products, which helped a bit. To really break through, they decided to take the tour to the next level. They not only changed the format to shift the focus to customer needs, they made sure all the customer's decision makers—from corporate facilities, finance, purchasing, human resources—were on the trip. They also hired trained facilitators to host the groups. These facilitators understood the products, but their real skill was identifying customer needs. They would start the program by asking the customers what they hoped to get out of the day. Often, each function would have a different objective, which created an opportunity for the sales teams to help align the executives on what they wanted and, in turn, find which of its own solutions best matched the customer's needs.

This approach proved so successful that the company has reengineered the customer visit down to the tiniest detail. The "what do you hope to get out of the day" session determines the day's agenda: if customers want to understand about innovation and technology, they are whisked off to the R&D lab; if they want to see the products in action, then they are shown how the company uses its own wares. Customers even preorder lunch so waiters won't interrupt mealtime conversation. Even the way the company's executives join in is tightly choreographed. With Disneyland-like precision a senior executive "bumps into" a group at a certain point on the facilities tour.

This may sound like an awful lot of effort. But, it is justifiable: more than half the prospects that visit end up as customers—more than double the win rate for bids that do not include a visit.

A maker of agricultural products found another creative way to involve its customers early in the sales process. It studied the buying patterns of farmers and realized that word of mouth played a major role in their buying decisions. But of course you need the right words out of the right mouths. It became clear that the biggest farmers set the trends and heavily influenced the buying habits of other farmers in the area. So the company developed its "lead user" program, selling its newest products to a few important farmers in each community. This provided early feedback on the product and created a loyal set of customers who would happily talk about its benefits, essentially preselling for the supplier.

To emphasize that its value proposition is solving the customer's business problem, a leading chemicals company trains sales reps not to mention the company's products in initial discussions. This goes against the grain—most salespeople want to move quickly to making an offer and closing—but

> "Advocating your product prematurely always leads to a price discussion later on."

it changes the dynamic and improves the outcome. "Advocating your product prematurely always leads to a price discussion later on," notes the head of sales. Starting with the customer needs gives the sales rep an opportunity to learn directly from the customer about their pain points and what they value in a solution, before putting on the table the products and services the company has to offer; a more aggressive sales pitch focused on specific products limits the scope of potential sales.

These examples all show that engaging the customer very early in the sales process allows companies to focus on customer needs as much as their own. This in turn gives customers a sense of ownership of products, which makes selling much easier. When a customer feels involved with a vendor's products or services, it improves loyalty, which in turn increases the vendor's share of wallet.

Bring your expertise to the table

Even the best products don't sell themselves and the more complex the product is, the more selling is about providing expertise. Leading sales executives have come to recognize this and are finding ways to use knowledge as a selling tool. They know that adding expertise to their sales teams can help them win additional business. For example, a McKinsey survey shows that consumer packaged goods companies that deploy more functional experts as part of their selling teams have higher than average category growth (Exhibit 9).

EXHIBIT 9

Winners in consumer packaged goods bring more experts to customers

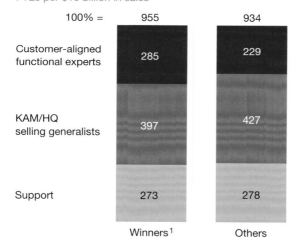

Selling resources in CPG companies
FTEs per $10 billion in sales

	Winners[1]	Others
100% =	955	934
Customer-aligned functional experts	285	229
KAM/HQ selling generalists	397	427
Support	273	278

1 Winners defined as higher than average category growth and better than average improvement in selling costs

A European telecommunications company decided to merge its mobile and fixed-line store networks to increase cross-selling between the two customer bases. It knew from the start that existing sales staff would not be able to sell the unfamiliar product unless the company radically simplified the portfolio, something it wanted to avoid.

Initially, the company tried training programs to build knowledge among store personnel, but these didn't deliver the results sales leaders wanted. So, they took a more innovative tack. First, they created "store rangers"—experts who would be fully conversant with either mobile or fixed-line options. The company created one team of rangers to cover all the stores in a particular territory. Every store would get a mobile solutions ranger for one or two days a week, and a wireless services ranger for a different one or two days. When in stores, the rangers would be very proactive, talking to clients and selling based on their expertise. This not only increased sales with those individual customers, but also provided on-the-job training for the full-time store salespeople.

A separate "virtual support" effort filled in when the appropriate ranger was not in the store. Using a videoconferencing setup, the store could bring in a live expert to talk directly to the customer. The remote expert could help the customer configure a new service, or even fill out paperwork. The in-store salesperson would be right there so the personal connection was not lost (Exhibit 10). Cross-sales took about a year to really ramp up, but eventually resulted in an increase in overall sales of more than 30 percent for the store network.

As we noted in the introduction to this section, lack of product or service knowledge is one of the most destructive kinds of sales experience. This is particularly true when it comes to B2B technology sales. Here's how one medical device company avoids that problem: "We always arrive in a bus," says a

> "It's never clear what the customer will really need, so 16 of us come, which guarantees that someone at the meeting can answer the customer's questions."

84

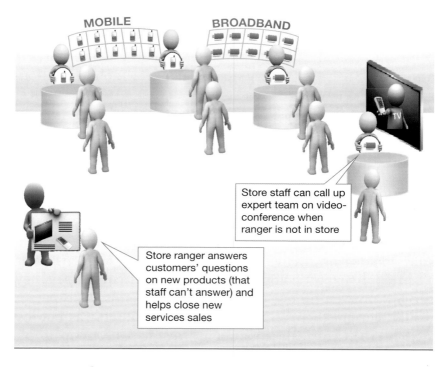

EXHIBIT 10

Store rangers help store staff cross-sell new telecommunications services

MOBILE

BROADBAND

Store staff can call up expert team on video-conference when ranger is not in store

Store ranger answers customers' questions on new products (that staff can't answer) and helps close new services sales

company sales rep. "It's never clear what the customer will really need, so 16 of us come, which guarantees that someone at the meeting can answer the customer's questions."

That's an extreme response to a common challenge; for most companies, it isn't cost-effective to drag large teams around to all customers on the off-chance that a question arises only one of them can answer. More often, leading companies have figured out ways to provide experts and technical support on an as-needed basis.

Bring expertise to key account management

How do you staff a dedicated key account team when the level of customer demand varies so much across the life cycle? A credit card issuer solved this problem by creating a flexible account management model that allowed it to temporarily add staff from a shared resources pool to boost capacity at critical times.

This redesign not only allowed the company to meet its top customers' needs cost-effectively, it actually made it possible to give key accounts a higher level of service using fewer resources. This led to increases in key account sales of 15 to 30 percent and invigorated the entire key account organization.

Here's how it works: each key account is assigned a permanent small core team that takes care of day-to-day account planning and support. When there is a specific need for expertise, such as during a contract renegotiation, the core team requests specialist support. These specialists come from a shared resources group and consist of high performers drawn from key accounts (account executives, contract negotiators, business analysts) and from functions (loyalty, legal, technology, market research, etc.). Once the tasks have been completed, they return to the pool to be redeployed elsewhere.

The core team may also be supported by roving teams also staffed from the specialist shared resources pool. These roving teams spend several months (or sometimes up to a year) rolling out new products or ideas sequentially across accounts. When the rollout is complete, the team disbands again.

Sales managers at an IT services provider established a centralized knowledge center staffed by experts that supports the sales force through a single point of access. It has three tiers of support: self-service access to best-in-class, standardized tools and support material such as pricing and total cost of ownership guidelines, standard contracts, etc.; phone and e-mail access to an expert, who can then pass the question to more specialized resources or "practice experts" if needed; and dedicated subject matter experts, who are accessible only through referral by the phone/e-mail experts. This structure gives sales leaders a clear idea of the nature of the demand for experts.

In addition, the company also set up "mega deal" teams that focus on the biggest sales opportunities at priority clients and prospects. At the core of the team is a small group of experts and specialists, so the biggest deals get dedicated subject matter experts, who also have experience working on precisely the sort of complex deals and competitive negotiations that were at stake.

Sales leaders at another company we interviewed took a different but equally successful approach to bringing expertise to customers. This industrial manufacturer had a long sales cycle as its big projects took months to negotiate and needed to step up its win rate on the very largest deals.

Its response was simple but highly effective. It set up a trigger in its CRM system: as soon as a salesperson entered an opportunity worth more than $100,000 (a sizeable deal for this company), an e-mail alert was sent to sales leaders in the company, including the business unit president. This had a powerful effect. Executives weighed in with their perspectives, contributing ideas on how to position the bid and suggesting which specialists would be required to win the sale. Based on this input, sales specialists, engineers, and other technical experts were deployed quickly. This collective effort to rally around the biggest opportunities doubled the company's win rate on large projects and was the catalyst to driving double-digit revenue growth.

Pursue new prospects relentlessly

Most sales organizations pursue growth by identifying and winning new customers. It is a perennial challenge for sales executives to keep their people in the hunt. Most sales models eventually turn hunters into farmers: a sales rep lands a big account and then gets paid commission on that account. Then, happy with the ongoing income, the rep has lost the hunger that motivates true hunters. Most compensation models enforce this behavior. Some companies try to make up for the hunter-to-farmer evolution by deploying dedicated hunters. That has its own challenges, such as getting compensation right and keeping dedicated hunters motivated.

Our interviews highlighted a number of examples where companies have overcome these hurdles and deployed effective hunting models. One European manufacturer was already a market leader thanks to its strong brand, a broad product line, and a large sales force. But it was finding it hard to grow further.

The company started with incentives for prospecting and asked staff to spend a certain percentage of their time on acquiring customers. Unfortunately, the demands of managing existing clients overwhelmed the orders and incentives. Then the company tried a dedicated hunting group, but this too proved unproductive.

> **Quarterly hunting days generated two months' worth of leads in a single day.**

After reflecting on what had gone wrong with these approaches, sales leaders tried a model built around "hunting days." Once a quarter, the entire sales force stepped away from their existing accounts and spent the entire day calling 8 to 10 new accounts per rep. The results were dramatic. In just a single day the sales force generated two months' worth of leads. The model was also sustainable, given that it used the existing sales force so there was no additional fixed investment.

Our interviews highlighted a number of other innovative ways in which companies are prospecting. A high-tech company carefully monitored changes of chief information officers in large corporations it did not serve and then aggressively pursued the new CIOs. It knew from experience that a change of management in an IT operation often leads to new selling opportunities.

A healthcare provider had success with the dedicated hunter model by requiring hunters to hand their new accounts over to farmer colleagues immediately. Many companies that try the dedicated hunter approach move the hunting rep off the account gradually, which causes confusion for the customer and, inevitably, poor morale among hunters. The healthcare company instead pitched the idea of bringing the account rep in at the end of the sales process as a positive thing. It assured customers that a dedicated account rep offered a better level of service than other suppliers could deliver, and indeed customers reacted very positively. This meant that hunters could get on with what they did best—finding new business.

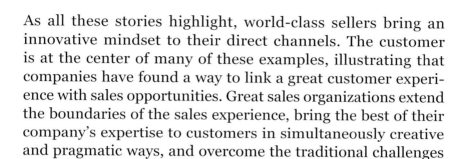

As all these stories highlight, world-class sellers bring an innovative mindset to their direct channels. The customer is at the center of many of these examples, illustrating that companies have found a way to link a great customer experience with sales opportunities. Great sales organizations extend the boundaries of the sales experience, bring the best of their company's expertise to customers in simultaneously creative and pragmatic ways, and overcome the traditional challenges that make prospecting difficult.

In the next chapter, we'll highlight how such companies take similarly innovative approaches with their indirect channels.

5. Invest in partners for mutual profit

"If we are together, nothing is impossible. If we are divided, all will fail."

—*Winston Churchill*

The executive general manager of an Asia-Pacific bank hung her head in frustration. Mortgage margins were shrinking across the industry as wholesale funding costs rose and rose. But her broker channel was resisting accepting lower commissions to bear its share of the pain.

To make matters worse, the bank was competing head-on with its own brokers. The bank needed brokers to capture the growing retail mortgage segment, so it had been signing them up. It recognized that customers believed this channel option gave them convenient access to products from multiple lenders and competitive pricing. However, it was never clear which customer segments would be targeted by internal staff and which by brokers. The result: duplication of effort and troubled broker relationships.

The general manager had to make this channel work. The bank was losing ground to competitors and couldn't afford to lose mortgages because of unmotivated or unhappy brokers. Brokers controlled 30 percent of the mortgage market and their share was growing. So was their influence, as consumers increasingly turned to brokers for a full suite of financial products.

Fast-forward six years: revenue from brokers has grown by 35 percent, brokers are cross-selling the bank's credit cards and insurance products at record rates, and the bank's declining share of the mortgage market is starting to rebound. Most importantly, broker feedback now shows the bank to be a partner of choice.

What changed? First, the bank stopped supporting the bottom quartile of brokers—the poorest performers—and focused on building stronger relationships with fewer, higher-performing brokers. Next, it met with major broker associations to explain why the existing compensation model was unsustainable and gained important commission concessions. (It helped that competitor banks were making the same demands.)

To soften the impact of lower commissions, bank leaders committed to lowering broker costs—but in a way that also benefited the bank's own bottom line. They streamlined the mortgage processing work flow to reduce handoffs and rework, then automated it to make it even more efficient. They addressed frontline productivity obstacles and, finally, took strides to address the channel conflict. This required making performance metrics the same for brokers and internal staff and changing compensation models to ensure brokers owned customer relationships and were still compensated for products that had to be sold through the bank for regulatory reasons.

It's a brave decision to revolutionize your relationship with partners. Brave, but necessary. As the bank's general manager saw, indirect channels are frequently the best way to reach important markets such as emerging economies or the fast-growing small and medium business (SMB) segment, which is too fragmented for most vendors to serve cost-effectively through direct channels. What's more, customers often want local expertise and service and the choice and convenience that multivendor, multicategory partners provide. As we saw with the automaker entering India in chapter 1, well-managed channel ecosystems can prove critical to market conquest.

> It's a brave decision to revolutionize your relationship with partners. Brave, but necessary.

Today, most companies employ indirect channels in some form as part of the multichannel model needed to sell their full range of products and services. But many have yet to maximize the opportunity that comes from striking the right balance between direct and indirect (as discussed in chapter 3) and to optimize channel partner performance (our focus here).

The central problem most companies face is that direct and indirect selling are fundamentally different business models. As the head of sales for a software company put it: "It's very difficult to do both direct and indirect selling well." Often, it's the channel management that proves difficult. Conflicts arise or vendor-partner relationships deteriorate into arm wrestling over slim margins and finger-pointing about who has failed to

94

bring sufficient value to the table (Exhibit 11). Once they take root, such tensions can take years to resolve.

EXHIBIT 11

Common misunderstandings in vendor-partner relationships

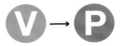

What vendors want from partners

Visibility—on market opportunity and customer insights

Vision for growth—plans and capabilities for growth segments

Effectiveness—expertise, knowledge of the portfolio

Added value—net new customers, ROI on partner investments

Clear roles—coordination between direct and indirect, distributors and resellers

What partners want from vendors

Better economics—margins, ROIC, vendor co-investment in growth

Simplification—fewer products, simpler partner programs

No duplication—of assets, partners, investments

Clear roles—target segments for partners vs. direct

Collaboration—on go-to-market planning

Support—tools, training

Channel optimization typically improves indirect revenues by 10 to 20 percent and reduces cost of sales by 5 to 10 percent.

Companies that master the challenge and avoid the pitfalls win big, improving channel revenues by 10 to 20 percent and reducing cost of sales by 5 to 10 percent. From our discussions and interviews, we find companies that excel at managing channels do two things well:

- **They manage partners as an extension of their sales force.** In contrast to the "hire and forget" approach to channel partners of some companies, leading sales organizations work as hard to improve their partners' performance as they do that of their own sales force. They don't see profits as a finite sum to be divided across the value chain but, rather, as a rising tide that can lift all boats together.

- **They confront channel conflict head-on.** Sales leaders spend considerable time engineering the right balance of competition and collaboration between channels. They also continuously challenge partners to raise their games or be cut from the program, and reward those who succeed with more support, training, etc. to propel them to the next level of performance.

Manage partners as an extension of your sales force

What does it mean to manage partners as an extension of your sales force? It means treating your indirect and direct organizations as interconnected resources and managing partners like—rather than differently from—their direct sales counterparts. In practical terms, it implies that you should know the strengths and weaknesses of your partners, make sure your partners' bottom line is healthy, and manage partners' performance as rigorously as you do your own sales team's.

Many companies start down the wrong path with partner channels by taking only a high-level view—all they want to know is if they have the right number of partner organizations in the right places to get coverage. A software company we know reminds us that it's more important to know who's on each partner team than how many teams are playing, particularly when it comes to selling complex solutions.

> Know the strengths and weaknesses of your partners, make sure your partners' bottom line is healthy, and manage partners' performance as rigorously as you do your own sales team's.

So, this company's sales leaders examine partner capabilities at a more granular level, looking at the number and types of roles within specific partner practices in specific regions and at the number of individuals certified to sell priority offerings—much as they do with their direct sales teams. With more intimate knowledge of the partner team, the software company can better appreciate how many deals each partner can handle and match capacity accordingly. More importantly, they can identify bottlenecks constraining growth (e.g., a shortage of specialists) and temporarily make internal resources available until the partner is able to hire or train.

A major risk in working with partners, of course, is not being able to control their behavior. Another software company found itself in a dilemma: its sales leaders applauded the entrepreneurial spirit of its highest performing "go-getter" partners, but found that their enthusiasm sometimes destroyed, rather than created, value. For example, when the company increased rebates to improve partner economics, the partners simply passed the savings along to customers to gain a price advantage and make sales, resulting in little bottom-line benefit to partner or supplier. Similarly, resellers aggressively pushed to carry the latest, greatest new technologies, worried they might miss out on the next big thing—and underestimated the effort required to get up to speed on new products. More importantly, by taking on products that weren't yet understood in the market, they assumed the heavy burden of educating customers and driving adoption. As resellers struggled with longer sales cycles and lower conversion on the new products, they lost focus on those established core products they were better able to sell, and thus revenues fell.

Sales leaders at the company resolved to design programs that would have a lasting impact on partners' as well as its own bottom line. It switched focus from rebates and product offerings to sales leads and conversion. On the leads side, the company's scale enabled it to identify and qualify new sales opportunities much more cost effectively than individual partners could. What's more, the investment to take a lead from "warm" to "hot" represented a smaller share of the software company's profit margin than the partner's. Consequently, by investing in more effective lead generation and qualification for partners, sales leaders were able to reduce partner costs significantly, while only slightly increasing their own.

To help the partners make the most of the leads, the company introduced new training programs to help partners run their business better—with courses on effective closing or working capital management, in addition to the usual product training. It also created marketing kits and other tools to make it easier for partners to sell higher margin services such as consulting. Finally, it improved some of its own processes. It resisted pressure to launch new products prematurely through reseller channels, and shifted the burden of building market awareness onto the direct sales force and internal services organization. As partners stayed focused on core products and their revenues improved, they recognized the wisdom of the software vendor's new policy of doing the "heavy lifting" itself.

By focusing on a broader set of economic incentives, rather than only traditional financial ones, the software company was able to get partners to focus on the profit drivers that the company wanted to rely on: selling higher margin services and solutions. In addition, sustained improvements to partner profitability built greater partner loyalty. Today, 90 percent of the company's partners build their businesses around the software company's products. Such a symbiotic relationship between vendor and partner can become a serious competitive advantage (see sidebar, "Supporting retailers makes sense for everyone").

As we will discuss in chapter 8, one of the most important differentiators of sales leaders is their highly-disciplined approach to performance management. The same is true for running partner sales teams.

The bank we met at the beginning of this chapter cut 2,500 partners as the first step in its channel redesign and segmented the remainder into five tiers based on performance; the higher the tier, the better the partner benefits, including larger territories. The sales executives at an equipment manufacturer did the same, rationalizing their top-tier partners from 6,000 to 3,500 and promoting and demoting partners from tier to tier each quarter based on revenues, commitment to growth objectives, and customer satisfaction.

In both companies, this discipline proved motivational, giving high-performing partners larger territories in which they could flex their muscles and less competition with other partners. For the equipment manufacturer, partner mindshare increased in line with the sales opportunities and the company shot to the top of the industry's "best channel vendor" rankings. The company, of course, also offers a rich set of growth-aligned incentives, including kickers for partners that identify opportunities with new customers, and exclusives and higher margins for partners targeting strategically important growth areas.

An Indian agricultural company learned the importance of building channel partner success in different ways. A new entrant attacked its distribution network, hurting sales. The regional sales director had painstakingly implemented an incentive program to exert last mile control over its extensive distribution and reseller network, but channel partners had begun stocking products from other suppliers and pricing was becoming undisciplined. To understand what was going wrong, the sales director spent a week with these partners to see the world through their eyes.

What he found was amazing. First, partner capabilities varied widely. Some were great at selling but poor at planning inventory and vice versa. Second, partners were excited and eager to work with vendors that would help them be successful. Third, the incentives the agricultural company was providing—primarily rebates and point-of-sale promotions—were too easily passed through to consumers and did not do anything to improve partner success. As a result, partners perceived the vendor as uncommitted.

The solution from there was obvious: more focus on "true partnership" with the right partners. The head of sales redefined the partner selection criteria and sought to recruit fewer, higher-caliber partners in which the company could invest more deeply. He hired a shadow sales

Deeper relationships with the right partners grew market share from 21 to 26 percent in 18 months.

Supporting retailers makes sense for everyone

At a time when most vendors were pushing as many costs as possible downstream, a leisure apparel company stood out as a supplier of choice by doing just the opposite. It collaborated with large retailers to take cost out of their systems and improve their overall economics.

First, recognizing that some of its retail partners lacked sophisticated inventory planning and logistics skills, it replaced its relationship-focused account managers with former retail buyers. These new reps had deep analytical skills and helped retailers determine how fast various categories were selling in order to guide purchasing decisions. There was a history of overpurchasing within the category, leading to surplus stock and margin-destroying markdowns. As the head of sales put it, some retailers can be like "fish in an aquarium: if something's selling, they'll eat until they die." So part of the rep's job was to save the retailers from themselves and prevent retailers from overbuying. It sounds counterintuitive to tell your customer to buy less, but it meant fewer markdowns and a fatter bottom line for the company and its partners.

Second, sales leaders implemented a buyback policy on slow-moving merchandise, which it could redirect to its own factory stores. Retailers could then invest in new product lines that they

could sell at or close to full price. To mitigate its risk, the company set guidelines on the types of product it would accept back. This program became a competitive weapon, which its rivals lacked the scale or mindset to replicate—again improving partner profitability and loyalty.

Finally, to improve joint performance, the company created a sales operations group whose members acted as part of the retail partner's organization, extending its own best practices to the partner (for example, aggregating and mining joint data for consumer insights). They also redesigned supply chains to ship more products directly from the factory to the retailer's distribution center or even the store, drastically reducing transportation costs; and provided an inside perspective on partner pain points, which helped prioritize sales, IT, and logistical investments. The program generated value three times its costs and clearly positioned the vendor as a partner-focused organization.

All these efforts paid off spectacularly. Curbing discounts improved profitability for the manufacture and the retailers. And, by proving it was committed to helping partners succeed, the supplier increased its share of wallet in its largest accounts from 20 percent—which had seemed unsustainably high at the time—to 60 to 70 percent over the course of ten years.

force that worked alongside new partners and coached them on day-to-day selling—building their confidence, reference cases, and accelerating time to productivity. Finally, the company committed to building deeper, more enduring relationships with these partners over time. The investment paid off: in just 18 months, improved partner performance grew the company's market share from 21 to 26 percent.

Confront channel conflict head-on

Virtually all the high-performing sales executives we spoke to described channel partners as perennially paranoid about vendors shifting business to their own direct sales forces or to another channel. While some channel partner fears are unfounded, some degree of channel conflict is inevitable and can breed healthy competition. But too much is both distracting and destructive, and the effects can be long-lasting.

> Some degree of channel conflict can breed healthy competition. But too much is both distracting and destructive, and the effects can be long-lasting.

With this in mind, sales leaders at a channel-focused software company trod carefully when they created a direct sales force to target the enterprise segment its partners weren't well positioned to serve. First, they presented a business case to partners: based on early sales data, every $1 the vendor earned in enterprise software sales generated $7 in partner revenues in the form of systems integration and other services for the enterprise account and products and services sold to the enterprise company's downstream customers.

Next, sales executives reduced areas of direct competition, particularly in services. They deliberately limited the company's service business to less than 10 percent of revenues, to ensure the business stayed focused on large accounts rather than poaching small businesses from partners. Again, they proactively communicated the benefit to partners. For example, they committed to relay service leads from smaller companies or opportunities that exceeded the company's service capacity to partners. The sales services group would be used to innovate selling practices, sharing successes with partners to improve their operations.

A global IT hardware company took a similar approach when it added an online channel to reach the small business segment its reseller partners served. To allay partners' fears, it marshaled data showing that very few partners sold to the subsegments targeted by the online channel—very small businesses that typically bought from retailers, rather than resellers. Further, it showed that those customers valued the convenience of purchasing online and would likely switch to online competitors if the hardware company didn't address their needs. Finally, the company identified the small subset of partners who would be affected and calculated their importance to the company. It then provided training, sales support, and marketing to help the best performers in this group refocus on other opportunities; lower priority partners who weren't hurt and/or were unable to hurt the vendor's business were left to move on.

It was clearly a smart move to acknowledge and communicate the risks and benefits of the new channel and help vulnerable partners that were worth retaining. The online channel now accounts for more than 10 percent of sales and the company has retained its excellent relations with resellers—remaining a supplier of choice, according to third-party surveys of high-tech resellers.

> Leaders take a pragmatic approach to recognizing where conflict is inevitable and thoughtfully mitigate the impact.

This is not to say that channel conflict is always easily managed. The objective is neither to eliminate tension nor to overmanage it (Exhibit 12). The best companies provide clarity and incentives to keep each channel focused on the areas where it can contribute most. They also take a pragmatic approach to recognizing where conflict is inevitable and thoughtfully mitigate the impact for those partners that have earned protection.

EXHIBIT 12

Ideas to mitigate channel conflict

Between direct sales and channel partners

Value cutoffs: direct sales owns accounts/deals above the line; partners below

Rules of engagement: target segments, timing to hand off new accounts

Incentives: referral bonuses, compensate everyone involved

Level playing field: same end-customer price through direct or indirect

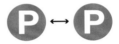

Between channel partners

Deal registration: first to claim the opportunity earns credit for the sale

Exclusives: geographic, product, segment, and territories

Selective intervention: heightened protection for priority partners

—————⊖—————

With sales leaders across industries relying more heavily on channel partners to reach new segments and regions, channel management is a fundamental requirement for sales success. The best practices described in this chapter are by no means comprehensive, but illustrate some of the most effective ways we saw of optimizing indirect channel performance. Companies that invest in channels and manage them as thoughtfully as they do their direct sales organizations are rewarded with higher performance and a source of competitive advantage.

Stu L. Levenick
Group President, Caterpillar

What makes Caterpillar's dealer model different?

We're about as close to a "handshake" model as it's possible to get in today's business world. It's a very long-standing approach that marries local dealers' independent entrepreneurial energy, culture, language and strong customer relationships with our global scale in technology and manufacturing expertise—both sides totally focused on satisfying the customer. The average Caterpillar dealer has been a partner for over 40 years. Some were dealers before Caterpillar was formed in 1925. It's very hard for our competitors to replicate that—indeed, our dealer network is our single biggest competitive advantage.

How do you work with dealers?

First of all, the dealers themselves vary. We work with a range of dealer ownership structures that spans small family-owned businesses to large public companies. None of them are franchises. They simply have the right to sell—and the responsibility to support—Caterpillar products. We have a simple sales and service agreement that can be cancelled by written notice—by either party, without cause.

We treat dealers as our equals. Right now, we have 188 dealers and we know them all on a first-name basis. There's a strong sense of mutual respect and mutual responsibility between us and them. We rely on them and very much want them to succeed and be viewed as very attractive businesses. Accordingly, we set very high expectations for them and our field teams work closely with them to ensure achievement. If a dealer is facing challenges, then we can draw on our background and global experiences to help address their needs.

There's a lot of communication between us and the dealers. We understand their business deeply and the key issues that impact performance and we work with them not only on short-term operational issues, but long-term dealer development and leadership continuity. We want all of our dealers to run a successful, customer-focused business. Occasionally a dealer leaves the network, but that's usually more to do with management or ownership continuity rather than performance. In the end, it's a marriage with each party committed to the other's success.

How do you help dealers?

We help them build their capabilities using our knowledge and experience with global best practices. We have substantial resources in the field, on the ground, working day to day on the issues necessary for their success. We don't actually invest financially in their businesses, but we provide knowledge and resources to help them develop their people and capabilities. We also bring them best practices. For example, we help them implement lean processes in their operations. In return they give us great connectivity to customers and insights to design better product and service innovations.

How do you avoid channel conflict?

It's simply not an issue. Our number one focus is the customer. Of course we have conversations with dealers, especially if we change things, but it's definitely a two-way conversation. For example, years ago our dealers were skeptical about the equipment rental business. However, we were convinced there was great potential there. It's turned into a major portion of our business and a great customer solution. Also, some years ago when we tried to implement a common ERP system with every dealer we got the message pretty quickly that this wasn't going to work, so we instead let them have system flexibility as long as the interfaces and processes met certain standards necessary to keep us well-aligned and integrated.

How have new technologies improved dealer operations?

Even when it comes to using the Internet, both Caterpillar and our dealers focus on helping customers first. We've come a long way from when dealers were truly local and data never crossed borders. Now it flows instantly everywhere. It's changed how we operate, but ultimately, the online channel enables dealers' relationships with customers.

A good example of leveraging technology took place at a recent trade show. At the show, registration information was populated into our Lead Capture application on the iPad. We also populated the application with relevant product information for the machines on display. As show workers engaged customers, they used the iPads to communicate product information—showing videos, etc.—

and to gather additional information about the customer, including purchase interest and follow-up requirements. Any literature the customer wanted was sent to the customer via the iPad. The captured lead information was then merged with the registration data and other customer information to help prioritize the leads before sending them to our dealers for follow-up. Prioritized leads were sent to our dealers the week following the show. Our contact center follows up with customers directly at 15 days, 90 days, 180 days, and 365 days to determine if the dealer has contacted them and if they have purchased products they expressed interest in at the show. This technology makes it much easier to have targeted conversations with prospects and feed these leads immediately back to the relevant dealers who would then follow up.

Part three:
Soup up your
sales engine

In the previous three chapters, we've looked at how world-class sales leaders can meet customers' needs and drive growth by optimizing individual channels and mastering multichannel sales. This doesn't come by waving a magic wand—underpinning all the great practices we've discussed are a high-performing sales operations team and supporting technology solutions.

The sales executives we spoke with have unlocked enormous value out of their sales operations. They have turned them into engines of growth—often from undermanaged, unproductive cost centers. They have also conquered the technology challenge and are harnessing information systems to get real frontline productivity and better customer experience.

In this section, we'll explore in more detail how great sales leaders have refocused their sales operations and IT investments to better serve their sales teams and ultimately their customers:

Chapter 6: Tune sales operations for growth highlights how leading sales organizations use sales operations to give reps more sales time and make the entire customer experience smoother.

Chapter 7: Build a technological advantage in sales looks at how these companies leverage IT in sales by giving sales teams the insights they need to be even more productive, enabling channel partners with better technology, and by engaging customers in new and exciting ways across digital channels.

6. Tune sales operations for growth

"We are what we repeatedly do. Excellence, then, is not an act, but a habit."

—Aristotle

Here's one for the record books: A sales team was so delighted by the increased productivity it experienced after the sales support function was reengineered that reps volunteered to give part of their bonuses to the support staff. Yes, that's right. The reps dug into their own pockets to show their gratitude.

You'd be grateful too, if you had lived through this global manufacturer's transformation. Sales operations had reached a stage where phone sales reps were spending 75 percent of their time away from the phones. They were trying to push through stalled deals, scurrying to find data to answer customer questions and cobbling together one-off proposals for even the simplest requests. Even highly paid field reps were spending almost half their time on internal sales support and tracking deal progress. In order to put a standard proposal together, reps had to coordinate meetings with as many as seven different people.

Often it took two to three weeks of constant effort for a field rep to get a special price approved.

This headache reached its climax during a product launch. The organization simply wasn't able to deliver the volume of time-sensitive proposals needed to nail down those critically important first orders. In addition, proposal quality varied dramatically across field reps. Some sent out spreadsheets with a simple price quote while others created 50-page documents, stressing value propositions that they had dreamed up on their own. This was not what senior management had in mind.

> The goal was simple: let sales reps sell, and let support staff support.

After this wake-up call, sales leaders decided it was time to act, and moved to separate sales from support. The goal was simple: let sales reps sell, and let support staff support. The company created "sales factories" comprised of specialized sales support staff with functional responsibility, and "deal coordinators" with back-office responsibility to shepherd deals through the system on behalf of the sales reps.

The company standardized internal sales processes and simplified interfaces between sales, customers, and manufacturing. It established clear service-level agreements for core support functions that spelled out what was required and a comprehensive performance management system that focused on speed and quality. The company also streamlined the proposal process, creating a library of proven pitch documents by product and by industry segment, which reps could quickly adapt rather than waste time writing them from scratch.

As the company rolled out the program country by country, the impact began to be felt—in some cases in as quickly as four months. Reps gained 15 percent more time for selling, there was a 5 percent improvement in win rates, and cycle time for internal sales processes shrank by 20 percent.

Even if these reps were unusual in their generous gesture towards their back-office colleagues, the results were actually fairly typical for a successful sales transformation. Sales leaders at other companies told us how optimizing sales operations across all channels led to revenue gains of 10 to 25 percent, even as standardization

> Optimizing sales operations can improve revenues by 10 to 25 percent and reduce back-office costs by 20 to 30 percent.

and other process improvements reduce back-office costs by 20 to 30 percent. For a major global player, the potential benefits can run into the hundreds of millions of dollars.

So, why haven't more companies overhauled sales operations to get these top- and bottom-line benefits? Many have yet to realize the extent of the opportunity. Pockets of sales support are hidden across divisions and locations—along with costs and redundancy. And management often has no idea just how much pain is inflicted on frontline sales staff and customers when sales operations are slow, overly complex, unresponsive, and inaccurate.

Our interviews and client experiences suggest that sales operations remains one of the biggest opportunities for improvement in SG&A, as well as a source of growth and differentiation. The first step toward realizing these gains is to get a comprehensive assessment of the current state of play.

118

EXHIBIT 13

A holistic definition of sales operations

Top sales leaders ask somebody in their direct team to assay the entire sales operations landscape—with the understanding that sales operations includes all non-quota carrying activities that support quota-carrying activities, extending beyond transactional tasks and including any activity that affects sales performance (Exhibit 13).

As sales leaders plan to optimize sales operations, they must also consider how actions taken in one area affect other parts of the sales organization. One risk is that centralization and standardization can go too far, undermining the ability of some divisions or sales departments to serve their customers. All sales operations can be improved, but not always in the same way.

The leading companies we spoke to focus on two areas of operations improvements to propel them to the next levels of sales excellence:

- **They give sales teams more time to sell.** Sales operations are crucial to releasing reps' time from non-selling activity; once they see the benefit of the change, their behavior becomes self-sustaining.

- **They use sales operations to customers' benefit.** Improving operations can have an enormous impact on customers. A smoother and faster sales process can boost loyalty, even if it may require some adaptations to customers' own operations.

Give sales teams more time to sell

When it comes to optimizing sales operations, the guiding principle for sales executives is to maximize time for selling and relationship building (Exhibit 14).[8] This sounds obvious, but it's critical to remember as the drive for effectiveness races against the forces of rising complexity. Growth and the proliferation of products and channels in both B2B and B2C continually reinject non-selling activities into the sales person's day. Winning back and protecting selling time, therefore, requires continuous vigilance.

Here's how one logistics company did it. As it plotted its comeback from the recession and tried to develop new growth initiatives, it surveyed its sales teams and found that only 35 percent of their time was spent actively selling, while six non-sales activities consumed nearly half their time. Billing system updates, firefighting, and internal communications were the chief time wasters.

---

8   Company analysis.

EXHIBIT 14

Optimizing sales operations increases selling time (telecoms example)

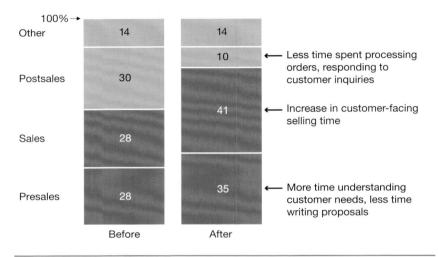

The sales managers analyzed the diaries of every rep to find the cause of each time sink, and convened cross-organizational teams to come up with solutions. They equipped the sales force with tools to automate and expedite pre-close activities (contract templates, automated pricing tools, etc.). Second, they outsourced dispute resolution and reassigned other non-sales activities such as billing and collection from the front line to the back office with clear rules and standard procedures. Finally, the company invested in customer self-serve tools that preempted inquiries to sales and support staff. The online system also helped internally, giving the customer service teams clear guidance on how to handle common issues. As a result, the company was able to maintain its workload with 25 percent fewer staff.

Once you have created more selling time, the trick is to defend it and make it permanent. Not only do new demands chip away at reps' selling time, so do ancient habits. Based on training and experience, a rep's reflex response is to drop everything and dive in when a customer demands a quick answer. These were good habits at one time, but are highly unproductive when a modern sales support mechanism is in place that can

Once you have created more selling time, the trick is to defend it and make it permanent.

handle the issue faster and better than the rep. "It is key to stop reps from bypassing the new system, even if they think they are more effective," says a top sales executive at the high-tech company. "Their time is better used to sell."

A European telecommunications company helped break the old habits by colocating sales operations teams with sales groups. Actually seeing the support staffer who was helping their customers and how well they performed engendered trust between sales and sales operations staff. Each customer and its sales rep were assigned a customer service person, whose photo and phone number they received. This service rep would answer customer calls 80 percent of the time (if they were away from their desk then another member of the customer care team would answer). Each sales group established clear roles and responsibilities to determine which requests went to sales and which to sales operations. The company also created formal service level agreements, specifying sales reps' minimum levels of satisfaction with their customer service rep. The increased selling time and back-office improvements significantly improved revenue at the telecommunications company, raising the value of contracts closed per week by 30 percent.

Finally, sales leaders reinforced the new model—and protected the expanded selling time—by setting aggressive activity targets,

Seizing a sales opportunity

When a global consumer products company began an ERP implementation for its international business, it quickly realized it would need to reinvent its sales processes as well if it was to realize the new system's potential. In Latin America—its largest international region—each country had developed its own sales support processes and many were using offline tools such as Excel that couldn't be accessed by other employees. The order-to-cash process was particularly problematic, since activities that were performed by sales in one country might be performed by finance in other. To complicate matters further, the company was seeking rapid growth in the range of 10 to 15 percent—it simply couldn't hire fast enough to keep pace with demand.

The sales leadership took a hard look in the mirror and decided to create selling capacity by tackling sales operations head on. It began by defining the activities and subactivities in its order-to-cash process, and determining the skill set needed to perform each one. Then it asked itself a series of questions: How important was local market knowledge to the task? How important was consistency across markets? Could the task be centralized or outsourced? It decided that tasks such as quoting should remain in-country,

while others, such as credit checking and service ordering, could be performed more efficiently at a centralized service center. The company then optimized and automated the individual process flows at each level of the organization.

In the process, the company freed up approximately 30 percent of sales support time, enabling employees to refocus on higher value activities they had never had the time to do, e.g., pricing strategy, customer planning, post-promotion analysis. Frontline sales reps were also happier: they could spend more time selling and less time making collection calls and troubleshooting. Perhaps most importantly, customers were happier: large retail customers now enjoyed a simplified, consistent experience across countries, instead of having to adapt to the vendor's country-specific selling process.

Sales leaders expect further improvements to customer experience as the ERP system comes online. For the time being, they are celebrating the major accomplishment of realizing growth without increasing the size of the sales organization.

such as for the number of new customer meetings reps needed to make. Targets were calibrated so that reps could not hit the numbers unless they stepped away from sales operations tasks and trusted the process to work. Once reps saw the process did in fact work, it created a self-reinforcing cycle—the more they stayed out of the support realm, the better they did.

Use sales operations to customers' benefit

Optimizing sales operations isn't purely for the vendor's benefit. It also has a direct positive impact on customer experience and can help retain and expand accounts. Tighter cycle times for proposals and queries, for example, translate into higher win rates and greater customer loyalty. A Fortune 50 company found that for every two days it cut from cycle time, it increased its win rate by 1 percent.

> A Fortune 50 company found that for every two days it cut from cycle time, it increased its win rate by 1 percent.

This all might seem obvious, but it doesn't mean that execution is always straightforward. For example, sales leaders we interviewed at a service provider had worked hard to reduce the time for various steps in the sales process, such as providing a quote or sending a completed contract. But, over the years, total cycle time actually expanded and customers grew frustrated with increasing delays. The head of sales operations told us: "I was getting calls from customers saying they were considering switching providers."

The root of the problem: Rather than optimize the end-to-end sales process, the company had focused on each individual step.

Unearthing investment opportunities

In addition to enabling growth and improving service, optimized sales operations significantly affect costs and the bottom line. As we mentioned, sales operations tend to be scattered and costs are tucked into unseen budgets, even in the best-run organizations. Over time, they can become cripplingly large. This was the case for a technology company, whose sales operations had become so fragmented that it no longer knew how much they cost. When it eventually added up the pieces it discovered sales operations comprised more than 5,000 people and cost more than $1 billion a year. Management was aghast. "If only we could redeploy a portion of that to sales growth!" said a senior sales executive.

The company found that it could. Like the services provider, it mapped the end-to-end process for a representative set of deals and identified more than 100 pain points that frequently caused deals to stall. Managers then ranked the relative importance of those pain points and developed initiatives to address the most critical ones. This information drove the redesign of sales operations, which included eliminating duplication, centralizing shared support activities such as contract administration, and standardizing IT infrastructure and interfaces. The payoff: more than 30 percent reduction in the sales operations budget, worth $300 million.

Employees were quick to close a ticket and hand off their work package with incomplete information, creating delay and rework when materials returned for completion. As a result, overall cycle time had grown and grown—even though it took less time to complete each step.

Before they lost any major customers, the head of sales operations set out to transform the back office. First, he asked a few major customers to act as an advisory board on process redesign. Then his team followed a sample of orders through every step of the process to see where the delays occurred. They soon discovered that 80 percent of sales operations efforts were consumed by deals worth just 20 percent of revenues.

The team solved the problem by segmenting deals by complexity and tailoring the process for each, to remove unnecessary steps and touches. For example, minor price changes no longer required going back through the full process. The personnel who were freed up from simpler deals were reallocated to the highly complex, large-value deals that really did require extensive customization and handholding. This effort improved cycle time for all the deals—including the most complex ones—by weeks and even months. By eliminating unnecessary steps, the company also cut the cost of sales operations by 15 percent. If companies are to maximize the potential captured from segmenting at the front line, this back-office segmentation is a critical step.

In this example, one of the key success factors was the customer advisory board, which provided feedback on every step of the improvement process. Importantly, for the new deal segmentation model to work, customers had to change their own internal processes to adapt to the standard interface on simpler deals and accept that not every deal needed the white-glove treatment. Customers benefitted financially from this change, too: one was able to reduce the resources dedicated to interacting with the service provider by 25 percent, which restored and enhanced customer loyalty.

———○———

It was clear from our conversations that improving sales operations has an enormous payoff. But it requires a high degree of commitment and organizational collaboration. In most large organizations, sales operations span multiple business units and geographies. Someone must compel leaders from across the organization to sit down, share data and be willing to talk about what's not working. Therefore, the effort requires a top leader who can override internal politics and keep a focus on what is the best solution, no matter what past practices have been.

Optimizing sales operations is also a continuous process, requiring new capabilities. New roles, skills, and behaviors are needed from the sales force to the back office—and even from customers. To make change stick, companies must stress collaboration and trust and redesign incentives to manage performance across the spectrum of sales activities. It is a tall order. But surely it is worth the effort.

In the next chapter we discuss ideas from leading sales executives to leverage technology to better enable sales teams, channel partners, and customers alike.

7. Build a technological advantage in sales

"Any sufficiently advanced technology is indistinguishable from magic."

—*Arthur C. Clarke*

In previous chapters, we have looked at a range of best practices—from identifying growth ahead of competition to mastering multiple routes to market, and managing sales operations to deliver frontline benefits. Executing all these initiatives requires information technology. As the search for growth becomes more challenging, as channels become more complex, and as customers become ever more sophisticated in their use of digital channels, IT systems will only become more central to outselling the competition.

Unfortunately, the history of IT in sales is a tale of mixed success. Even among the companies we interviewed for this book, only about two thirds report real frontline improvements from IT investments. The other third say they spend a lot but gain little other than frustration. Too often, when sales management systems were introduced, reps became bogged down in data, or couldn't get the right data. That has to change. Companies can no longer afford to make wasteful investments—they need to get good at using technology to compete and to drive growth.

> When companies get technology right, the results can be impressive.

When companies get technology right, the results can be impressive. Capital One, for example, developed a unique customer profiling system that mined transaction data from individual customers to generate personally customized marketing and sales approaches. Capital One's customer acquisition rate was five times better than the industry average over years.

What are companies that maximize the returns on their IT investments doing right? Based on our interviews, we found that they are using technology to succeed on three fronts:

- **They arm the sales team with insights.** Giving reps on the ground and in the office the tools to make them more productive and effective is vital in maximizing sales potential.

- **They enable channel partners.** Treating partners as an extension of the sales force; they make sure they have the right collaboration tools to improve the flow of data between the two organizations.

- **They improve the customer experience using digital channels.** Customers are becoming ever more comfortable and confident with online and mobile channels for all stages of the sales journey. The smartest companies are responding with some innovative ways to use these digital technologies.

Arm the sales team

The difference between success and frustration with IT often depends on how easily the company can turn technological advances into insights that sales teams can use in competition. The insights can come from some new software applications, through detailed customer analytics, or through buzz on social media.

A global consumer goods player had a scattered sales force that spent its time on the road visiting small independent retailers. Sales leaders used technology to improve reps' productivity in two ways. First, they used data on store hours, traffic conditions, and the optimal time to visit each customer to develop daily route maps for reps. No longer did reps have to waste time figuring out their own routes—they just picked up the maps every morning.

When they got to the stores, a second bit of technology helped reps quickly and accurately monitor how their products were displayed. Reps would take pictures of the displays with digital cameras, then upload them to a central system with a leading-edge photo-recognition software program that automatically identifies the goods labels. The system then tells the rep whether the shop owner had stocked the display cases correctly—and if shop owners had placed competitor products in the branded display units in violation of their agreements. After the system was introduced, sales from these smaller retailers rose 10 percent partly due to this program, and the average revenue per account increased, too.

The system made the cumbersome but crucial task of monitoring displays very simple for the sales rep and made it easy for them to explain to store owners how the correct display boosted sales and profitability. It also allowed for new, more effective sales rep performance indicators. Rather than evaluating reps solely on volume, sales managers now had tools to measure how well reps were helping store owners maximize sales.

For a North American building materials supplier, a technology overhaul helped revive the art of selling. When the recession hit and construction came to a near-standstill, the company took stock and decided to rethink its sales strategy. Sales leaders felt that the company had lost its selling skills during the boom when orders simply flowed in and now—during the bust, when every sale was contested—its investments in web-based sales support and CRM tools were not delivering results.

The head of sales set two goals for the new IT system. First, to allocate sales capacity to the best opportunities and, second, generate closing pitches for the sales team, generating the right value proposition for each type of customer, including retention offers for customers at risk.

In retrospect, the company says the most important step in its success was starting with clearly articulated requirements and then making clear to the IT specialists exactly what they expected the system to do. Then it collaborated with the IT vendors to create the right systems to support these activities.

The first step in implementation was to create a list of best prospects based on an "ideal customer" profile, which was derived from the order histories of customers with which the company had near 100 percent penetration. The profile included factors such as size and industry sector. It then refined the list by using a churn predictor based on order patterns of customers just before they stopped being customers. The profiles helped identify where the company could increase its share, head off a defection, or admit defeat and allocate resources more productively.

Using a sales force automation tool, the company translated

> A list of best prospects was based on an "ideal customer" profile, which was derived from the order histories of customers with which the company had near 100 percent penetration.

the customer profiling data into actionable sales plans. Sales leaders segmented customers into four groups based on their degree of fit with the ideal template. Each segment was assigned a different call frequency rate, with the best prospects getting the most attention and the loosest fits receiving the least. The system also told reps which products to offer, based on sales histories that included the relative penetration of different categories and products. The reports also suggested best pitches tied to the next-products-to-sell list for each customer. Finally, the system flagged at-risk accounts and told reps to arrange immediate face-to-face visits, equipping them with targeted value propositions to try and avoid losing the customer.

The IT system greatly improved the sales teams' pitches because it selected the right value proposition based on real insights gained from sales people who had actually participated in sales calls at similar customers. This was a huge improvement over pitched developed purely by marketing or product specialists. Average annual earnings grew by 3 to 5 percent as a result of this program.

Enable channel partners

In chapter 5, we saw the benefits of treating channel partners as an extension of the company's sales force. In this spirit, the best sales organizations have extended their own IT systems to partners. Among other services, they provide partners with finely-tuned prospecting lists and support for managing sales rep performance.

> The best sales organizations have extended their own IT systems to partners.

High-tech company Cisco became a leader in sharing tools with partners after it got its own sales house in order (see sidebar)[9]. Before launching this new approach, it faced the same complaints that many companies hear from resellers: the deal registration process was a headache, deal reviews and approvals were slow, and channel partners would argue they were losing deals as a result.

So Cisco opened its suite of communications tools to channel partners. Now, when a partner's rep registers a deal on Cisco's portal he or she can see immediately if their contact person is available to approve the deal on the spot. If the account manager is on the road, the rep can leave a voicemail with all the details. This is then converted to text, which makes it simpler for the manager to accept, decline, or transmit to the next approver. The approver can even add a voicemail to inform the rep of the decision. All this can be done from the rep's mobile phone.

---

9   "Transforming Sales Operations with Collaboration", Cisco white paper.

Even high-tech sales organizations need better IT

As a leader in communication technology, Cisco decided to use its own IT expertise to raise the effectiveness of its sales organization. Cisco sales leaders found that valuable sales time was being wasted on trivial tasks; lengthy backroom processes were hindering efficiency and customers couldn't get the information they needed to finalize a buying decision. They decided to address these issues head on:

Selling time: Sales reps were spending up to 90 minutes each day playing phone tag. Now, everyone in the company is connected to an advanced instant messaging system that integrates calendar and location functions so reps can easily find the right person to answer any question at any time.

Expertise: Product specialists, a scarce resource, were spending half their day answering basic product questions, restricting the time they had to attend the product demos that often clinch a sale. Now, customers can attend virtual demos and quiz the experts through an online conference portal. Customers love the convenience, and the company has dramatically improved its specialists' productivity as they can now speak to far more customers every day.

Partner support: Activities such as approvals and reviews were slow—it could take up to two weeks for a Cisco reseller to get a deal approved. Using the new portal, partners get all the access to data and communication support that Cisco direct sale reps have.

In pilots, these tools alone enabled account managers to generate 3 percent higher average sales than the rest of Cisco sales force. It did not take Cisco long to decide to deploy such systems and tools across the company.

Another global high-tech company, SAP, has also innovated the approach to partner interactions. In 2011, the software supplier launched a collaborative tool that makes it easy to create customer/partner communities online. On the SAP website, a customer can search the full range of SAP solutions and see which channel partners to contact for different solutions. The website also hosts chat areas for partners where it encourages them to get to know each other better and develop alliances to go after new opportunities—extending the capabilities and performance potential of both parties.

An office products company we spoke to used point-of-sale data from its retailer partners combined with syndicated sales-out market data, and using its analytics capabilities to better understand consumer buying behavior in specific markets. This helped it coach partners on more effective ways to capitalize on promotion, price, product and placement, but also enabled collaboration in supply chain management, and logistics. Both the company and its retailers achieved double-digit profit growth in the targeted categories in effectively flat markets. In addition, the company received various "Vendor of the Year" awards.

To help partners improve sales forecasting and performance management, sales executives at the industrial products manufacturer we discussed in chapter 4 decided to co-fund CRM tools for each distributor. To be eligible for commissions, the distributor had to input their sales pipelines into the system. But the inputs were kept simple and there was just one access point per distributor. "This created the initial benefit of giving us visibility into the sales pipeline. However, the bigger benefit is that distributors became much more disciplined about boosting their own sales pipelines," said the head of sales.

Improve the customer experience

Using technology to improve customer experience will be a growing focus of IT efforts for many companies. In a 2010 McKinsey survey of chief marketing and sales officers, two-thirds said e-commerce and multichannel sales will be "important or very important" to the success of their companies. Almost three-quarters felt the same way about online and digital marketing.

The Web is crammed with consumer information and surveys show an increasing number of purchasers research and evaluate products online, even if they wind up buying in a store. But this is not only a B2C phenomenon. In fact, business buyers surpass consumers when it comes to researching products on blogs, RSS feeds, forums, and rating sites.[10] And three-quarters of B2B buyers use social media as part of their research process.[11] Proprietary McKinsey research suggests that B2B customers would welcome the chance to use electronic channels and self-service tools even more.

> Business buyers surpass consumers when it comes to researching products on blogs, RSS feeds, forums, and rating sites.

Digital channels offer a host of financial benefits—not least a lower cost route to market. Perhaps most importantly, however, they help companies meet their customers' expectations. The best sales organizations are responding to these expectations and business opportunities by taking advantage of the unique capabilities of digital channels.

---

10   Forrester, *When to socialize online with B2B buyers*, December 2010.
11   ITSMA/PAC *How customers choose*, 2009 study.

One of the most important capabilities is capturing direct, unfiltered consumer feedback from the Internet. Several leading-edge sales executives told us they are investing in ways to harvest insights from social media. By "listening" to the chatter about their products, their competitors and the concerns of consumers on social media sites, these companies say they get much higher quality input than by surveys alone because the questions do not always elicit full responses or anticipate sudden changes in sentiment.

For example, when a health and beauty products company asked consumers their top concerns regarding diapers, more than two-thirds said they wanted environmentally friendly products. Sounded reasonable. Except this didn't resonate with the head of sales because it wasn't what she was hearing from her retail clients and some consumers. So she insisted the marketing team take a closer look at what consumers were actually saying online. A deeper look into the social media conversations revealed that the terms that most often cropped up in online conversations about the company's diapers were actually "organic" and "diaper rash." The company reacted by building parents' desire to protect their children from diaper rash by positioning the healthy, natural product into its product design and value proposition, and trained its sales force to use the social media insights to gain more shelf space at retailers.

Another digital channel that is gaining traction is mobile. Consumers use their mobile phones more and more as part of their decision journeys as they evaluate products and, with mobile payment systems, they are even beginning to use phones for purchasing (Exhibit 15).[12] This opens a whole new range of possibilities for improving customer experience at the point of sale for sellers.

12   McKinsey & Company iConsumer survey.

EXHIBIT 15

Mobile devices becoming part of consumer decision journey

2010 survey of 1,000+ US consumers

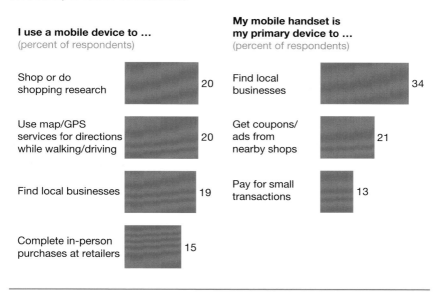

I use a mobile device to ...
(percent of respondents)

Shop or do shopping research	20
Use map/GPS services for directions while walking/driving	20
Find local businesses	19
Complete in-person purchases at retailers	15

My mobile handset is my primary device to ...
(percent of respondents)

Find local businesses	34
Get coupons/ ads from nearby shops	21
Pay for small transactions	13

Best Buy, for example, has added quick response (QR) codes near product placements in all its US retail stores. These codes can be scanned by any smart phone, which then provides a link to more detailed information about the product's features. This makes it much easier, for example, for shoppers to compare camera features such as the number of megapixels, type of memory card, etc. It also gives information on the average customer rating that the product has received. There are a host of similar phone-based tools that push more sales data to customers, and we are starting to see more location-specific coupons and discount offers sent to mobile phones to drive impulse sales.

In addition to helping sales leaders gather important insights about purchasing decisions, social media is being used to generate sales. For example, in London's Westfield shopping mall, retail technology specialist Nedap installed a "Twitter Mirror" during a major mall-wide promotional event. Customers could try on clothes and then have the mirror capture an image of them and post it on their Facebook pages and Twitter timelines for real-time feedback from their friends.

In a similar vein, a B2B electronics company we interviewed is harnessing online technology to drive sales directly with a suite of tools that let customers compile their own customized orders and still get the correct pricing online. The system allows them to change a wide variety of variables such as configuration and batching, in order to optimize price. Once orders have been placed, customers can change specifications as often as they like, and they immediately see the impact of those changes on price. The tools also allow them to see how the manufacture of their order is progressing. Anecdotally, customers have expressed greater satisfaction. As important, it has taken some of the burden of customer hand-holding away from reps who are now free to pursue new prospects.

As companies engage customers and partners through digital channels and touch points, they have to maintain a consistent customer experience offline and online. To achieve that, the world's best sales organizations have often taken "sales beyond sales" by making each component of their organization, from product design to sales to customer service and operations (e.g., internal IT department) see itself as contributing to the customer experience, so that together they coordinate customer experience delivery across multiple channels.

———◦———

Top sales organizations have used technology to improve their own operations, to support channel partners, and to enrich the customer experience. So much data is now available and can be processed and disseminated that the best sales executives are moving fast to keep up, without plunging into heavy investments with no clear ROI. They need to take a more strategic view of where to invest in IT and most importantly how to optimize the return on IT in sales.

Frank van Veenendaal
President, Worldwide Sales & Services,
Salesforce.com

What is your view on the future of digital sales channels?
What are the new elements that you see in how customers
will buy?

With digital channels, we have shifted from traditional
sales and marketing vehicles to a more social and viral
approach. We use YouTube videos to announce new
products and features. We invite bloggers to our events,
to generate online buzz. We have a group tracking tweets
and we're able to track our awareness at an individual
level and to understand what key influencers say about
us and our competitors online. We track where individuals
go after visiting our website and place targeted banner
ads on those sites. All told, digital channels enable us
to target individual decision makers rather than entire
customer organizations.

What role will social networks play in the sales process?

Social networks are evolving from a consumer to an
enterprise play, fundamentally changing how we drive
customer experience and sales. Our future prospects and
customers are more likely to look to Facebook and YouTube
for information than call our free number. Social networks
have replaced external market research in many ways as
trusted sources of referrals. We need to not just understand
what's being said about us in the social world, but shape

those perceptions. We use Radian 6 to listen to, measure, and engage our customers and prospects in this social world. Social tools have definitely helped us reach more of our addressable market and drive more demand than we could have through traditional sales channels alone. The trick is to get those channels working together. For example, telemarketing plays a key role for us, passing Web leads to sales teams for follow-up.

How has technology improved your sales team's performance?

We use our own technology to enable our business processes. In addition to our core CRM offering, we have a collaboration service called Salesforce Chatter that takes conversations that used to happen over e-mail, phone, and meetings, and makes them available to a broader set of people through feeds and private groups, similar to Facebook. In a sales context, this means that everyone interacting with a customer has access to that customer's full history—recent conversations, service calls, etc., no matter which part of our organization they connected with. If I'm preparing for a customer visit, I just look at the Chatter feed associated with the account to understand the current context and challenges, and I'm ready to go.

Chatter also improves our internal visibility. It helps reps navigate our network of experts, to quickly find the right person to answer any question. It connects sales and customer service in a way that is both art and science. And it helps me understand the health of different parts of my organization, which includes thousands of people across five levels of management—in a way that I never could over e-mail.

Internally, the collaboration benefits have cut conference calls, meetings, and e-mail volumes by 20 to 30 percent, freeing up time to focus on selling. Externally, our technology enables us to combine the scale of a large company with the flexibility and agility of a start-up, dramatically improving our value proposition.

How do you ensure your organization adopts the use of technology to drive a differentiated customer experience?

First and foremost, salesforce.com executives lead by example, communicating via Chatter whenever possible. Second, we publish best practices on how to use Chatter to drive business productivity. With good use cases in hand, people can better visualize the tool's benefits and potential. Third, we reward and acknowledge contributors since by design this is an opt-in tool. In a typical organization or even on social media, only 10 percent of readers actually contribute new content. At our company, that's closer to 50 percent. Our employees have really embraced these tools' collaborative value.

Part four:
It's all about you
and your people

A book about how the best sales leaders in the world meet the complex challenges of driving growth would not be complete without talking about those leaders themselves. The hidden theme behind all the success stories in the preceding chapters is outstanding sales leadership and investment in people, from the top of the organization to the front line and the back office.

A sales leader can have all the market analysis, all the multichannel processes, and all the technological wizardry but without the right talent, it will not achieve much. The executives we spoke to were keenly aware of this and invested significant personal time in ensuring they get the best out of their sales force. Indeed, when asked, performance management, capability building, and leadership came out as the most important skills their organizations had developed for long-term success:

Chapter 8: Manage performance for growth. Performance management, specifically setting the quota and associated compensation plan of the sales rep, is the bedrock of many sales organizations. However, we heard stories from leaders that went beyond these traditional carrots and sticks. They talked about tapping into deeper motivations beyond pay to unlock the true power of their sellers and also about creating a sense of pace and community around performance goals that quickly become part of the culture.

Chapter 9: Build sales DNA. While short-term performance is critical, the best sellers are thinking about the long-term health of their organization. They take the long view, balancing today's goal attainment with long-term capability building. The best sellers put extra energy into helping bring out the best in sales managers, who are the people who really make change happen in the field. Top companies also understand the importance of talent and are constantly looking for opportunities to upgrade.

Chapter 10: Growth starts at the very top. The 110 sales executives we met are a diverse group of leaders. Yet they all play an inspiring role in driving the success of their team. They challenge the status quo, they galvanize their team, they role model change, and they demand results beyond and above everything else.

8. Manage performance for growth

"I hear and I forget. I see and I remember. I do and I understand."

— Confucius

TDC, Denmark's incumbent telecommunications company, was finding growth challenging. One cause was obvious: aggressive attackers were making serious inroads. Less obvious was the internal roadblock to growth—a sales organization that was increasingly ineffective against the attackers.

In its quest for growth, TDC examined its sales performance to discover the root causes of its problems. In its B2B division, it found enormous variations between sales staff's performance: the number of customer meetings per account manager varied by a factor of 10 across the company and in some districts, reps had failed to call up to 60 percent of accounts, leaving the field wide open for the competition. Results were below management expectations and sales force morale and motivation were low.

Armed with this knowledge, the head of sales launched 14-week pilots to see how the company could perform better and more consistently at both the team and the individual rep level. Groups of ten sales reps were brought together, each under a team leader. Representatives from customer care and consulting also joined these teams. Teams were given a set of ten tools to use in their day-to-day work—all geared towards raising sales performance. These included daily hands-on coaching of the rep by the manager, checklists, frequent discussions of team and individual performance, and the use of a large "team board," on which each rep would record his or her weekly performance against targets. To help reps focus on the new tools, sales managers committed to remove any issues that hindered selling.

Every morning during the pilot the managers would run through the day's priorities with each rep and together they would brainstorm any challenges. The team board (Exhibit 16) showed the number of sales calls completed and the number of sales made for each rep. In weekly meetings, managers would provide additional coaching and the team would plot its strategy for the week ahead. The team board was based on a template provided by management, but it could be customized to suit groups' needs—some added margin and pricing metrics, others skills they needed for more complicated sales, and another measured team morale.

The results of the first pilots exceeded all aspirations. Sales calls per rep rose by 40 percent (the company simultaneously mandated daily call reporting in all locations, which yielded a 17 percent jump in calls outside the pilot offices). In pilot

EXHIBIT 16

Sales team performance board at TDC

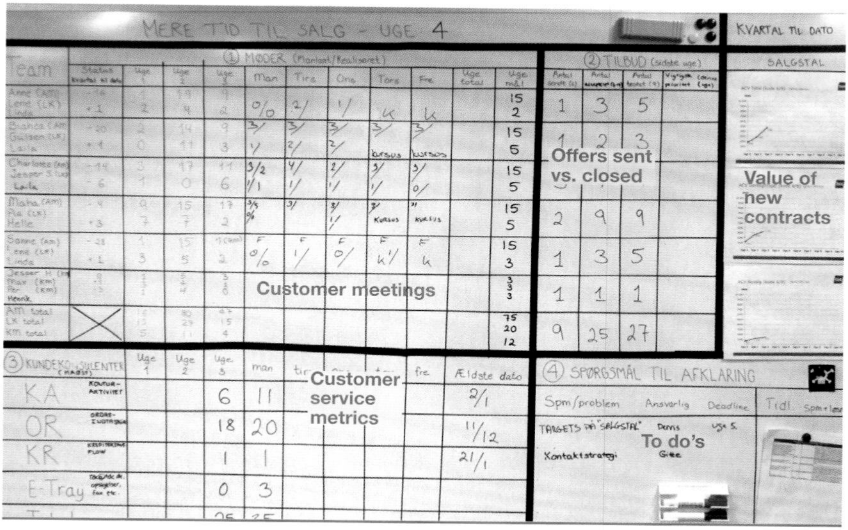

territories, offers closed per sales team rocketed by 75 percent, while average contract value per week rose by 80 percent—and by as much as 150 percent for new deals. In addition, variability of customer meetings per account manager shrank from a factor of 10 to just 3.5. These results were achieved with the same sales reps and managers who had been dragging TDC down. What had changed was the company's approach to sales performance management.

Given these extraordinary results, the head of B2B sales decided to roll out the program (dubbed TDC 2.0, a new way of working—see sidebar) across all districts over six months with similarly impressive results: in what was a challenging market, total contract value per week rose by 30 percent and customer satisfaction improved by 6 percentage points. Perhaps more important for sustained success, salespeople felt they had a better sense of direction and were more engaged with the top management's vision. They said that the pilots had inspired them to work to their full potential, and therefore they felt more satisfied with their work. They also made more money. The B2B sales team became the poster child for TDC's new way of working, inspiring the B2C sales group, and teams right across company.

TDC's starting point is not that uncommon. Across industries, we often find large variations in sales performance that cannot be just explained by legitimate sources of variability such as differences in tenure or business mix covered by the sales rep (Exhibit 17).

EXHIBIT 17

Sales performance varies by a factor of 2 to 4

Field sales: Sales rep performance can vary by a factor of 3 between top and bottom quartile, adjusted for tenure in similar districts

Telesales: Agents have a higher turnover than field reps, which accentuates performance variations. Sales performance varies by a factor of 2 between top and bottom quartile reps adjusted for tenure

Retail stores: Store employee performance productivity varies by a factor of 3 to 4, primarily because of store traffic. But performance management also plays a role, the amount of time that store managers spend on the floor correlates with frontline performance (i.e., when management is visible, sales performance improves)

Leading sales organizations have taken similar initiatives to TDC's to manage performance for growth. They understand the root causes of such performance variations, and they treat the sales force as capable adults who can learn and improve together and grow as a team. These companies also leave nothing to

A look inside TDC 2.0: interview with Martin Lippert, CEO, TDC Business, on TDC's new way of working

What is the most profound impact of TDC 2.0?

We operate with a higher clock-speed and are more in-sync. Our sales managers and employees focus on the most important opportunities. They are much more goal-oriented.

How has TDC 2.0 changed your sales team culture?

We came from a culture where we looked at our sales team performance in aggregate only. Now, we celebrate personal ambition and achievement. Personal development through manager coaching is a hallmark of how we run our business.

How has TDC 2.0 changed sales managers' role?

The manager role has changed completely from project managers to people mangers. Managers used to spend most of their time coordinating with other managers and were the "guest star of the week" in their department. Now they are the "daily manager—every day". This has changed our approach to manager recruiting, training, appraisal, and renewal.

Changing minds and behaviors is not easy. What would you do differently if you had to start over?

After one year, TDC 2.0 has become an ingrained part of the way we work. If I had to start over, I would communicate more broadly the program rationale and ambition at inception. I would also recruit more change agents (we call them "navigators") up-front. And lastly, I would make performance measurement and reporting easier from the start.

chance when it comes to performance management and do three things particularly well:

- **They coach rookies into rainmakers.** Coaching lies at the very heart of the success of leading sales organizations, and companies with any aspirations of excellence must move from seeing it as a "nice to have" to a core component of sales management.

- **They set the tempo of performance.** Regular reporting can be immensely powerful and ensures that the sales function is operating as effectively as possible from top to bottom.

- **They recognize it's not just about pay.** People are motivated in all manner of ways and the sales executives we spoke to talked more about peer approval and public recognition than compensation models.

Coach rookies into rainmakers

Unlocking a person's potential to maximize his or her own performance is about helping them to learn rather than teaching them. This form of coaching is critical in sales because adults learn best through "experiential" learning—i.e., by doing. Studies have shown that adults retain 65 percent of experiential learning compared to just 10 percent of material they receive in a lecture setting or in demonstrations.[13]

> Adults retain 65 percent of experiential training versus just 10 percent in a lecture or presentation.

---

13 IBM research; *John Whitmore Coaching for Performance: Growing People, Performance and Purpose,* Nicholas Brealey, 3rd edition, 2002.

Turning sales managers into coaches requires a change in behavior. At TDC, managers went from spending two to three hours a week coaching, to devoting around ten hours a week. In other top sales organizations, managers spend upwards of 60 percent of their time on coaching. What's more, coaching objectives and requirements are now a major focus of their annual evaluations.

For example, at an industrial company that we interviewed, the head of sales established an "80/80" rule: sales managers are expected to spend 80 percent of their time with sales reps, and 80 percent of their variable compensation is linked to that. By tying compensation to coaching, the head of sales sent a very strong signal as to the importance he attached to coaching for the success of the sales organization.

Based on our interviews with sales executives, it is clear that a structured coaching program with at least weekly contact between coach and sales rep is critically important. For example, a consumer services company mandates that sales managers conduct daily 15-minute check-in calls with all reps who fail to hit their monthly targets. Reps who make their target get weekly one-on-one sessions, and reps who exceed their target get a 10-minute praise call every week.

To reinforce best practices, the company requires managers to join each rep for a day every month. To make the most of these "ride-alongs", sales managers are trained to identify the causes of underperformance, feed back their findings, and recommend action plans. The bottom performers also spend a day on the road with a top-performing sales rep so they can really see what makes these stars stand apart.

The company also took a multipronged approach to improving its sales managers' coaching skills. It provided managers with training on traditional skills, such as handling difficult conversations. It also allocated a "super coach" to each sales manager. These coaches, drawn from its central sales training team, observed real-life coaching interactions between managers and sales reps, and gave specific feedback on their coaching skills. The company saw a very impressive result from its sales program, with a 25 percent improvement in close rates, and attributes its ability to execute and maintain impact to the coaching role of the sales manager.

Set the tempo of performance

When asked what the single biggest benefit of TDC's new way of working was, the CEO replied that "it raised the 'clock speed' of our sales team." Teams came together once or twice a week to review their progress against the plan, and discuss corrective actions.

> The head of sales convenes his worldwide sales leaders every Monday afternoon and goes through their pipelines.

This regular pace of reporting is important because it drives the tempo of the entire sales organization. At an industrial company, the head of sales convenes his worldwide sales leaders every Monday afternoon and goes through their pipelines using field data. This might seem like micromanaging, but he believes that the signals from this weekly meeting cascade through the entire sales organization, ensuring that everyone keeps pace with the company's aspirations.

EXHIBIT 18

Pace of performance management

Weekly sales calls at all levels of the organization

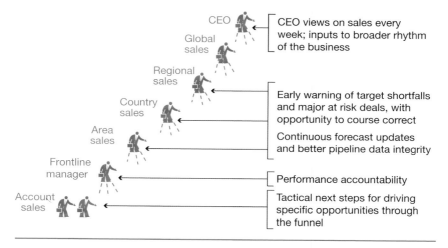

CEO — CEO views on sales every week; inputs to broader rhythm of the business

Global sales

Regional sales

Country sales — Early warning of target shortfalls and major at risk deals, with opportunity to course correct

Area sales — Continuous forecast updates and better pipeline data integrity

Frontline manager — Performance accountability

Account sales — Tactical next steps for driving specific opportunities through the funnel

Consider now the case of a high-tech company. Its performance management has a weekly rhythm. Every week, frontline sales reps call managers; managers call sales executives; and the top sales executive reports to the CEO—every single week. These calls generate action. Sales management scrutinizes performance and intervenes to coach, to solve a problem, or to raise a forecast—week in, week out (Exhibit 18).

Beyond setting the pace, sales leaders also use analytical tools and metrics to identify and address obstacles to sales success and to manage performance at a very granular level. "It is a myth that great sales leaders motivate through charisma and influence. Energy, pace, and enthusiasm are important, and great sales leaders run their operations with the precision of an engineering firm," says the head of advisor sales at a US financial services firm.

Best-practice sales organizations use simple but comprehensive reporting that allows them to drive performance at the account, consumer segment, individual sales unit, or product level. The data brings accountability to performance and lets them avoid guesswork when steering sales activities. Equally important, they avoid the trap of asking for reports on everything under the sun, which can backfire by diverting managers and sales reps from beneficial activities such as coaching and spending time with customers.

The best reports include leading and lagging indicators, metrics that increase the visibility of the performance at the individual rep (and, if possible, transaction) level and that cascade through all relevant levels in the organization. The data should give management immediate insight into what's working and what's not. "If we're not performing the way we'd like, we go straight to the metrics to see what is falling behind," the sales leader at a North American industrial company told us.

It's not just about pay

There is more to sales motivation than money. Many sales executives we spoke to agreed that while a company must get compensation right, it is not enough to drive lasting performance. As a head of sales at a financial advisory firm said, "Compensation might produce a short-term boost, but it won't sustainably improve sales. You have to tap into something deeper." That deeper source of motivation for financial advisors, he says, is helping clients achieve their financial goals. So, when an advisor isn't reaching his or her full potential, managers sit down with them. "We go through

> "Compensation might produce a short-term boost, but it won't sustainably improve sales."

the metrics to see where they need to make improvements to reach their aspirations," he added. "Together, we identify the things that will address the problems, including training, coaching, tools, help from others, new products, etc."

Another company told us that it motivates and inspires its star performers not by paying them more—they already make plenty—but rather by inviting them to share their lessons from the road with the entire sales organization. As part of its annual sales convention, the company asks these top sales people to give a plenary speech and to facilitate breakouts for colleagues. Such visibility seems to inspire the stars to return to the podium next year—they become the best coaches and the best motivation for others to learn winning behavior.

We have shown the extent to which performance management is a critical component of any sales growth program. But, while many companies focus relentlessly on short-term performance, leading sales organizations make investments in the long-term health of their sales force, developing sales capabilities and adapting the very DNA of their sales teams. This is how they manage to survive today and thrive tomorrow, and is the focus of our next chapter.

Mario Weiss

Executive Vice-President, Würth

*How do you approach performance management
in sales?*

Our motto is that good performance is compensated well,
extraordinary performance is compensated extraordinarily.
Performance alone is what propels people upwards at
Würth and sales performance is the beating heart of the
company. All other functions support the sales force. This is
the culture that Professor Reinhold Würth created decades
ago, and that gives us still a clear direction.

How does Würth go about coaching sales reps?

Our area managers are the most important people for
coaching. They are our "champions of success". They
have direct contact to the sales force and thus mold reps'
behavior. Each area manager has 10 to 15 direct reports,
and the main sales rep training method we use is "ride
alongs", where the area manager spends a whole day
with his sales rep, accompanying him in his daily work
at customers and giving him immediate feedback and
new input. The area managers actually spend 80 percent
of their time doing this, and it is this close involvement
with reps that drives the insights managers bring and
ultimately improves performance. We prepare our area
managers according to our worldwide standard "Learn
to Lead" program for exactly this task, and to ensure our
Würth standards of direct sales.

It's vital that these managers have high emotional intelligence in order to provide constructive criticism of reps' performance. Obviously we also have to train our area managers, which we do through "Learn to Lead" training modules that instill leadership principles, feedback and coaching techniques, and help with when and how to intervene in a negotiation.

How do you create performance transparency and accountability?

Our guiding principle is that reps should assume entrepreneurial responsibility. We have a decentralized organization and there is no micro-managing from head office. In fact we only have two planned dates: when we commit annual targets, and when we do the half-yearly milestone checkpoint. Our philosophy is that the more successful a sales team or company is, the more freedom we are willing to give it. We have no interest in interfering when things are going well. Of course, if a team is struggling to make its targets, which is controlled monthly, then head office will interfere, provide support and get the sales figures reported daily. Again it's Professor Würth's principle: "The greater the success, the more freedom and liberty!"

How do you motivate your sales force?

We believe in recognizing and rewarding excellence. The top 2 percent of performers become part of an elite group, and members get a one-week trip with their partners to the Caribbean or other dream destinations. We are very transparent about who the best reps are and we communicate very clearly that striving to be average is not good enough. We need people who want to influence their salaries, and we need people who want to be the best so while we provide the right environment and motivational tools, hiring the right people whose motivation fits to our requirements is vitally important.

How do you balance short- and long-term performance?

We expect sales reps to become customer managers. We provide standard, automated tools to help them manage the whole sales process and ensure we are giving customers as much value as possible. For example, we can tell customers which of their mechanics care for their equipment, which mechanic performs best and most efficiently or we offer our customers complete concepts and ideas on how to grow their business and profits. This helps build customer loyalty and turns one-off sales into continuous relationships, which are much more valuable and ensure long-term success. Knowing and understanding our customers are our biggest assets.

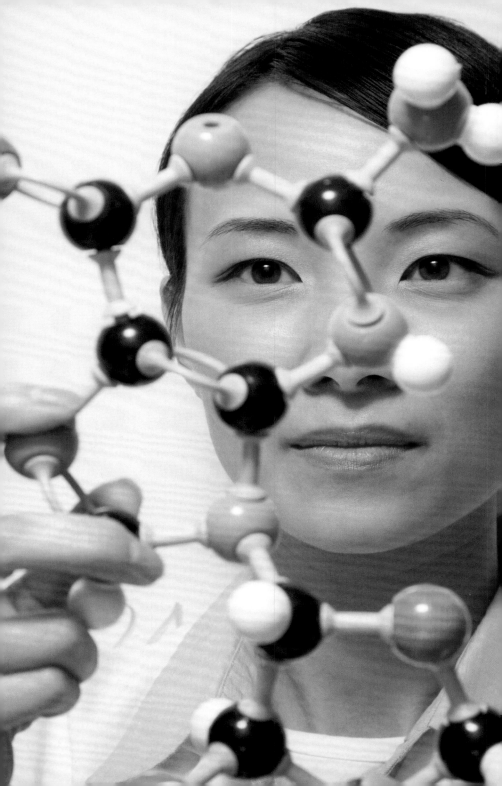

9. Build sales DNA

"It always seems impossible until it's done."

— Nelson Mandela

You can't change your personal DNA. The genetic code you are born with is what you are stuck with. It determines the color of your eyes and whether you're left- or right-handed. It even plays a part in how you will develop and function.

Fortunately, what is predetermined in an individual can be "recoded" in an organization. The ingredients that make a high-functioning sales organization—the most effective management behaviors and the required employee capabilities and mindsets—can be introduced, enhanced, and modified.

As a result, you can create the organizational "DNA" that makes successful selling second nature. Why does this matter? Less than a third of change programs and transformation efforts reach their performance targets. A staggering 70 percent of these failures are due to the organization's inability to quickly and completely adopt required new behavior, not because the initiatives were substandard.[14] Having the DNA in place—the right people with the right capabilities, motivation, and attitude—gives the organization the ability to align, execute, and renew faster than the competition. This is not just an important part of sustaining excellence, it's a precondition.

The story of a North American consumer services company is instructive. It tried for years to transform the performance of its field sales organization, rolling out a parade of sales stimulation programs—everything from unfocused prospecting programs to top-down corporate training initiatives. Few programs yielded more than incremental improvements and often gains in pilot markets faded with time.

The head of sales rethought the approach. This time, instead of focusing solely on what the sales force had to do, the program also devoted significant attention to building the talents and capabilities to enable them to do it. The embedded culture was highly independent: 2,000 reps across some 200 offices worked on an entirely commission-based compensation model. The company needed to fix the wide variation in rep performance.

The strategy was to raise productivity by standardizing on the proven best practices used by the highest performing reps. But to do that, the company would need to break down the old pattern of behavior—solo operators doing their own thing to get results their own ways. Research showed that the most important determinants of success among the top reps were their prospecting and selling approaches, and the way the reps articulated the company's value proposition. As we will detail

---

14   Michael Beer & Nitin Nohria, eds. *Breaking the Code of Change*, Boston: Harvard Business School Press, 2000.

below, the company made a substantial investment to teach these skills and enforced their use with specific goals.

The impact was enormous: a 25 percent improvement in rep productivity across all regions within 18 months. More impressive still, the gains stuck and two years later performance was still improving. The program was so successful that the company has rolled it out for its small business sales force and parts of its enterprise business. We shall look at how it achieved this success throughout this chapter.

> The impact was enormous: a 25 percent improvement in rep productivity across all regions within 18 months.

The company is not alone in concluding that real change requires new DNA—new capabilities and an organization that can adapt and evolve. Across nearly all of our interviews, building capabilities was a common theme and was most often cited as the top priority for driving growth—even ahead of selling the way customers want or improving sales back-office support.

Based on our research and interviews, we see three themes common to all organizations that have successfully lifted performance by building sales DNA:

- **They create a culture for the long term.** All great sales organizations have made it a priority to pursue long-term performance improvement—not just hitting short-term targets. They reach this goal by weaving capability-building into daily, weekly, and monthly routines to ensure that the focus never slips.

- **They give middle managers a starring role.** These are pivotal actors in building sales capabilities. These managers are the agents of change and reinforce frontline transformations. Investing here gives you the biggest bang for your buck and ensures improvements are embedded into the DNA.

- **They put together the A-team.** Successful sales leaders don't just focus on improving the capabilities of the existing team; they continuously seek to upgrade the people themselves. This is not limited to recruitment; it includes other people processes, such as initial training, promotion, and attrition.

Create a culture for the long term

Continuous improvement has become second nature in most operational functions. It's time to bring the same mindset to sales. The barriers to creating a continuous improvement mindset are substantial. Sales leaders have to deal with large, distributed teams and front lines that have a very short-term focus, which is driven by (important) quarterly quotas and targets. Moreover there is a perception that sales is more an art than science, which means that reps and managers who believe this will likely resist change.

> Capability-building efforts were seen as non-essential because they were not tied to the company's strategic objectives and did not help reps hit performance goals.

So, how do you get sales teams to embrace continuous improvement? The answer lies in how you approach capability building. The effort must be led by the right people—credible members of the sales establishment—and the training must be appropriate to adult learners who prize independence and entrepreneurialism. Based on our interviews, more than half of all capability-building efforts generate no return, largely because they are not well tailored to the needs of the trainees. They were seen as non-essential because they were not tied to the company's strategic objectives and did not help reps hit performance goals based on those objectives.

One driver of the consumer services company's sudden success was the way in which it chose to build the necessary capabilities. Sales leaders designed an eight-week implementation program for each geographic market. Each new skill was introduced in sequence, allowing reps to digest each one and to ensure that they stuck. To do this, the company used a "field and forum" approach. Frontline personnel, who were selected as trainers, came together for in-person training sessions where they learned about a new skill and then delivered the training in the field. At the next forum, the same group would return to share their experiences and knowledge and to learn the next program module.

The approach also tapped into principles of adult learning and motivation that we touched on in the previous chapter. Instead of the traditional conference call kickoff, handover of a playbook and a single visit from the training team, this program included in-person sales academies for managers, mandatory rep certifications, experiential learning and e-learning modules. Leading companies use regression analyses of rep performance, time observations on the ground, and 360-degree feedback data to determine training priorities, and thus the most appropriate learning approach.

Role playing is particularly important in building capabilities and is a technique that all the high-performing sales organizations we encountered use intensively. This is particularly important for improving the softer skills such as navigating difficult conversations. One high-tech player, for example, uses regular deal rehearsals in front of sales managers and other senior executives to create a culture of coaching and to use rehearsal to build muscle memory for reps so they can reflexively articulate the company's value proposition. A market research company we interviewed uses role playing and shadowing to ensure the most critical selling skills are "burned in." For less critical skills, such as remembering product facts, it relies on e-learning.

> Adults need to apply a new skill at least 20 times before it becomes second nature.

Once you have introduced a new skill, reinforcement is critical. Adults need to apply a new skill at least 20 times before it becomes second nature. At the consumer services company, sales leaders ensured compliance by reviewing calendars to track whether managers were scheduling coaching sessions with their reps, and checking updates and reasons for not closing deals. By tracking frontline behavior, management was able to intervene wherever it detected back-sliding in the field.

Most important, the company made enforcing the new behavior routine. It developed a model to guide weekly and monthly coaching and development conversations, which sales leaders described this as the most critical piece of the entire program—the glue that held it all together. By using regular coaching conversations about long-term performance goals based on the new skills with sales managers (and clearly separating those from short-term goals), the company constantly pushes reps to improve, even when senior management is not looking over their shoulders.

Finally, the company set long-range inspirational performance targets to make clear just how much improvement sales leaders expected. Reps were told that they would need to double prospecting performance. Not surprisingly, there was resistance to this "impossible" target, but the company stuck to its guns and found that these long-term targets were enormously powerful. They encouraged development conversations that focused on more than what was required to meet weekly, monthly, or quarterly sales targets; they acted as a constant reminder of the need to keep improving, even for those who were already high performers. Three years later the "impossible" was within reach of the entire sales force.

Give middle managers a starring role

Sales executives we spoke to emphasized that if you really want to transform sales organizations, your most important players are first- and second-line managers. They interact with reps daily and constantly reinforce good or bad behaviors. They are the role models that the troops respect and act as the change agents for a transformation. If these frontline managers provide coaching and support to inculcate new behaviors and processes, transformations take root. Too often, organizations underinvest in these managers and undermine the success of rep training.

> Too often, organizations underinvest in frontline managers and undermine the success of rep training.

When corporate-driven capability building programs failed to "stick" in the field, one software company enlisted the front line to drive the process. High performing managers and reps served on advisory councils to shape new initiatives, then owned the delivery and success of those programs in their respective geographies. When well-respected frontline leaders were the architects and advocates of change, new ideas took better hold, and the exposure that initiative owners gained accelerated their careers.

Danish telecommunications company TDC, which we discussed in the previous chapter, assigns a "navigator" to every manager to help identify local improvement opportunities and provide regular coaching. In effect, the sales managers were trained to become local change leaders. They were then far more effective at establishing and sustaining the transformation than any staff brought in from head office. Not only did the program delivered impressive growth (as discussed in chapter 8), it also drove a 10 percent improvement in the sales unit's internal "organizational health" scores (a measure of organizational functionality that includes factors such as speed of decision making and employee satisfaction).

At the consumer services company, sales managers used to be completely removed from rep training. While a trainer ran reps through their drills and passed on valuable knowledge, the sales manager would be holed up in his office with no idea of the content of that conversation. As soon as the company realized this oversight, it brought managers into the training process, which allows them to talk to the reps about what they have learned and reinforce the new skills as part of daily rep supervision (Exhibit 19).

Like sales reps, many sales managers can be resistant to a more "scientific" approach to improving sales performance. The sales leadership at the software company put a great deal of effort into building a culture of leadership among managers to ensure the right role-modeling and coaching took place. It assigned a "super coach" to every manager, who acted as mentors. They sat in on coaching sessions, reviewed performance results, and graded the area sales managers' progress. After successfully implementing

EXHIBIT 19
Giving middle managers a starring role

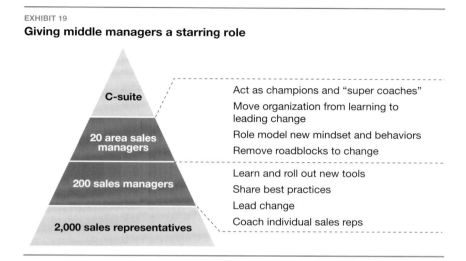

C-suite	Act as champions and "super coaches"
	Move organization from learning to leading change
20 area sales managers	Role model new mindset and behaviors
	Remove roadblocks to change
200 sales managers	Learn and roll out new tools
	Share best practices
	Lead change
2,000 sales representatives	Coach individual sales reps

the transformation in one or two offices under the guidance of their super coaches, area sales managers could then fly solo (including running their own sales academies).

Not only did this increase the speed and traction of the program, it also made first- and second-line managers feel better equipped to do their jobs. Manager attrition fell by 30 percent over two years.

Put together the A-team

Building capabilities can have a dramatic impact on the success of performance-improvement programs. But at some point, your progress is limited by the caliber of your teams. Ultimately, continuous improvement also requires upgrading the quality of people, not just their performance. "Get the right individual in the right role" was a common refrain during our interviews with leading sales leaders. These leaders invested more money and time in talent management—hiring the right people and managing their careers.

> As early as four months into the job, it was possible to see the kind of performer a new hire would be for the rest of his or her career.

In a second phase of its sales transformation, the North American consumer services company turned its attention to the quality of its sales force. It began by examining how performance changed over time and soon saw something startling: As early as four months into the job, it was possible to see the kind of performer a new hire will be for the rest of his or her career. In other words, if they don't show a knack for selling or the ability to learn right away, they never will. But it was customary for managers to give new reps a free pass for the first 12 months, assuming that this was their development phase and performance expectations should be lower. The company used this insight to accelerate the "develop vs. move on" decision.

The company also provided better support for new hires to make sure they had the chance to shine. It created a six-month new-hires program to ensure managers engaged early with new recruits and helped them perform to their full potential. The impact was impressive. By quickly eliminating the less promising new hires and saving on wages and hiring bounties, the company reduced recruitment costs by 45 percent. Management attention was focused on new reps who had the most potential and revenues even rose by up to 3 percent as leads went to young reps who had better close rates.

Other companies have attacked the talent problem by investing in ways to predict success even before a hiring decision is made. A chemical company, for example, built detailed hiring profiles containing both obvious sales rep attributes, such as a technical background and evidence of commercial drive, and less intuitive factors, such as a background as a college athlete, which they found to be a reliable predictor of personal drive.

Top companies also recognize that all sales roles are not the same and require slightly different talents. In addition, sales roles more broadly are evolving from account managers to problem solvers, as we've seen in chapter 4.

A high-tech firm learned this the hard way when it launched a new coverage model. The company had divided reps into one of three functions: direct sales, channel-led sales or hunting, but the pilot

> The best-performing sellers don't always turn out to be the best managers.

had mixed results. So senior managers consulted the local sales leaders, who quickly pinpointed the problem: they had simply put the wrong reps in the wrong roles. Some reps were not well suited to working with channel partners where the skills required were closer to those of sales management than traditional direct selling; others were not resilient enough to perform in the less structured, higher-risk hunting role. After taking an inventory of the existing reps, defining target skill sets and closing the capability gaps, they reassigned staff. This unlocked the underlying potential of the new coverage model and secured 10 to 15 percent growth.

Getting the right individual in the right role is especially important in sales management. Too often the best sales rep gets promoted into the job—only to find that the skills required to succeed as a manager are quite different. Indeed, the best performing sellers rarely turn out to be the best managers.

To develop sales leaders, a US financial institution has created a systematic approach for identifying future leaders. Very early on, every rep is assessed on these critical indicators of leadership: Are they capable and above average? Are they respected by others? Those who rate a check in both boxes are given assignments to test their capabilities further, such as running training programs or mentoring other reps. They are assessed against a rigorous four-part leadership model that does not include sales performance. Instead, the relevant metrics are covering relationships, people, strategy, and thought leadership. This gives the company a rich, qualified talent pipeline for succession planning.

It is just as important to keep strong producers who are not cut out for management on board. So many top sales organizations deliberately are creating alternative career paths for sales stars. One software company now elevates its best account managers to the same level as general managers, with compensation to match and commensurate titles. An IT hardware company uses financial and non-financial incentives (e.g., paid MBAs) to induce high performing frontline managers to spend an extra year or two in role.

> Forced attrition during a major transformation typically runs at least 10 to 20 percent.

Inevitably, getting the right individual in the right role also requires getting the wrong individuals out. Healthy renewal is a challenging but essential step in building sales DNA. Forced attrition during a major transformation typically runs at least 10 to 20 percent as you weed out those reps and managers who can't—or won't—make the change. One company we talked to targets a forced attrition rate of 6 to 8 percent, even in the best of times.

Over the course of a few years, this "refreshing" can make a real difference. For example, the head of sales at a market research company used talent management to drive a major business transformation. Realizing that the business was evolving and becoming more solutions-oriented, he saw that his sales force would not be credible with the kinds of clients who would be choosing solutions vendors.

First, he hired former management consultants who could effectively engage with customers on business problem solving and trained them to sell. When he found he could not hire quality talent fast enough to meet growth aspirations, he committed to developing the next generation of sales leaders internally. He overinvested in the high performers, creating mentoring programs and stretch development opportunities to accelerate their career advancement. He also consistently managed out the bottom 10 percent, to minimize resource investment in low performers. Four years later, the faces in sales meetings were completely different, but so were the numbers—revenues more than doubled.

———o———

Your opportunities are only as good as your organization's capabilities and outstanding sales performance refers as much to the fundamental caliber of your organization as it does to what you ask them to do. The sales leaders we interviewed have grasped this and invested accordingly. The result: real, sustained performance improvements.

This journey is not easy. As we will see in the following chapter, it requires strong personal leadership.

10. Growth starts at the very top

"Setting an example is not the main means of influencing others; it is the only means."

— *Albert Einstein*

In this book, we have shared real-life experiences of more than 110 sales executives about how their companies drive sales growth. We have distilled these into nine big ideas that we believe sales organizations should use today to raise their growth trajectories.

All these ideas would come to nothing without the courage, drive, imagination, and dedication of the sales executives themselves. During the course of researching this book, we learned a great deal about sales leadership—how each of these 110 men and women set a vision, inspired action, transformed organizations, and propelled growth in their companies.

> Transformations are more than 2.5 times as likely to succeed if they have strong leadership commitment.

This chapter is dedicated to them. We explore the role of the senior sales leader in driving growth. Strong leadership is a prerequisite for success. A 2010 survey shows that transformations of all kinds are more than 2.5 times as likely to succeed if they have strong leadership commitment. The executives we interviewed acknowledged that what they do—how they set the tone, show the vision and motivate—is essential in driving growth. They believe that sales growth starts at the top. We know it.

Effective sales leaders share a common set of approaches:

- **They challenge the status quo.** Great sales leaders seek opportunities to do business differently—anticipating and preempting customer pain points, and relentlessly pursuing a better sales experience for their customers.

- **They galvanize their teams.** The quickest way to send shock waves through a sales organization is for leaders to communicate one or two symbolic objectives the organization should pursue—and then stay on message.

- **They are the role models for change.** Organizations don't just change because the bosses want them to. Leaders must set the direction and make clear what is expected, but they are most persuasive when they walk the walk—demonstrating by their own actions what the new norm is.

- **They demand results, results, results.** Where significant customer impact is at stake, there is no substitute for the sales leader rolling up his or her sleeves and getting personally involved to deliver results ahead of competition.

Challenge the status quo

The story of Will, global head of sales at a high-tech company, is a good illustration of a leader pushing his organization to rethink the way it serves customers.

When Will started thinking about how to serve customers differently, his company's direct sales force was second to none, and in the enterprise segments, it set the industry standard. But he was not satisfied with the status quo—he had a long-term view of how to serve customers better, particularly in emerging and fast-growing markets. Specifically, he believed the company's direct sales forces should work with channel partners to expand its footprint in the enterprise segment. The company had worked with channel partners to serve small and mid-size customers. But direct sales had always had sole responsibility for enterprise sales and was understandably proud and protective.

> He had a long-term view of how to serve customers better, particularly in emerging and fast-growing markets.

No leader wants to upset a successful, powerful sales organization, but Will saw that growth was more important than preserving the status quo. He decided to grant channel partners a license to hunt freely for enterprise customers in fast-growing markets and asked sales leaders in four countries to pilot a program to let partners sell enterprise solutions on their own, with targeted support from the company's direct sales force. The sales leaders' reaction was predictable. They said it was too risky and that would lead to these accounts being lost. They argued that some partners didn't even have the right capabilities to win these deals and the company's competitors would have a field day. They also worried that this approach would hurt the company's margins.

If their pessimism had proved accurate we wouldn't be telling you this story. After one year, this new model produced amazing results. In those countries that adopted Will's new approach, growth soared to 25 percent year-on-year. And far from damaging margins, they actually rose by a few points.

By challenging the status quo and received sales wisdom, Will sent a clear message to his sales leaders: they, too, should always question their ways of doing business with customers and partners—to see what lucrative new opportunities might exist.

Galvanize your team

Consider the case of Neil, the CEO of a national telecommunications operator in an emerging market. One day, he astonished his leadership team by announcing a bold "3x3x3" growth aspiration: three years to expand beyond his home country, three years to expand beyond his region, and three years to become a leading global brand. By articulating his goals so simply, he painted an inspiring picture of the journey ahead that everyone could understand, and also broke the long-term goal into medium-term steps that were easy to understand—individually exciting, and easily measurable.

> He painted an inspiring picture of the journey ahead that everyone could understand.

Seven years later, when the company's operations had reached over 20 countries across multiple continents, Neil wanted all employees, and the outside world, to have the same understanding of what this company stood for. He challenged his team to develop a compelling, innovative, and emotionally engaging way to articulate the company's aspiration. His team came up with the idea of using the notion of a "new birth" as the analogy for the company's new life. The team wrote a short memo in the style of a child telling the world what she wanted to become when she grew up, what moved her, and what her "promise" to the world was. This was captured in a movie, where a 7-year-old girl read the letter out aloud from an empty stage under a single spotlight. The video was broadcast simultaneously to the top 400 managers at a major launch event, and e-mailed to all employees. Many seasoned executives reportedly left the meeting with tears in their eyes, after a standing ovation.

Neil's story is a good example of how a compelling vision and strong emotional leadership can galvanize a team towards very ambitious growth goals. Once he has his growth story, Neil seized every opportunity to talk about it with employees, reinforcing what the story was about, drawing out its relevance to different parts of the business, and prompting sales reps to find their own personal meanings.

Be the role model for change

Consider now the case of Philippe, head of sales of a telecommunications operator in a western European market. He is credited with having built a very successful retail network over the past decade as well as for creating an online and self-service sales channel ahead of competition.

> He had to be the change he wanted to see in his team.

Yet, Philippe wanted to be known not only for his company's effective go-to-market strategy, but as the industry benchmark in customer's sales experience both in store and online. He knew that customer experience was crucial to keep customers and avoid churn. He had also learned that customer sales experience in stores and on the web was almost as important as network quality to his customers.

Philippe had spent his entire career in sales and channel organizations. He decided that if he wanted to convince others of his vision of becoming the market leader in customer experience (an idea typically advocated by marketing or customer service) he had to "be the change" he wanted to see in his team. He was a big believer in leading by example because he knew his sales staff scrutinized every move he made and everything he said, so he proposed to his CEO that customer experience should determine 25 percent of his variable pay and that of his direct reports.

Philippe also believed in taking few simple actions to reinforce unequivocally the importance of customer experience. While reviewing the individual performance of his store managers, he realized that aggressive selling can actually harm customer experience. Therefore, he controversially decided to cap the number of sales transactions in his stores. Sales managers could never recall such action, although it was more symbolic than an attempt to really constrain them.

Although at first, sales staff found the notion counterintuitive. Soon, however, they realized that it meant they could spend more quality time with customers and understand their needs. This was good not only for that all-important customer experience, but also led to more upselling so that in fact revenues actually improved under this model.

Philippe also made a particular effort to personalize the change he wanted to see, talking about his experience in his company's store. In his discussions with his team, he would ask himself questions like "How does this relate to me?", "Why does it matter to me personally?" and shared his views with others.

Demand results, results, results!

Laura is the North America head of sales for a consumer packaged goods company. She inherited a strong brand and good customer relationships when she took over her job. But her first instinct was that there was still room to grow. From day one, she started working with her team, aligning on a collective aspiration for growth.

Her sales team quickly got to know her as somebody who places a very high bar on performance. They also recognized that she had the energy and passion to help them achieve that performance. While she was competitive and focused on customers (and spent a lot of time out of her office meeting them), she

> She placed a very high bar on performance and had the passion and energy to help her team deliver.

was not a relationship leader. But, because she was aware of her own blind spots, she favored leaders on her team who were relationship developers.

In her drive for the best sales results possible, Laura focused on two simple ideas with her team. First, she made sure roles and responsibilities for growth were completely clear, down and across her organization. She insisted on one point of accountability to make clear who was accountable for important activities. Two, she was rigorous at moving talent around in her organization to reward high performers and position them to drive growth.

Laura had been in the trenches and used stories from her own experience as a frontline sales rep to inspire her team. She asked direct questions to get to know accounts inside-out and participated in forecast calls, asking probing questions to and followed up with resources and investments to pursue opportunities. No detail was too small. In another context, Laura might have been perceived as an overly controlling micro-manager. But her team responded positively because she had credibility and they saw that she matched her high demands for performance with her own passion and drive and was willing to collaborate to help her team win.

Because the most senior sales leaders set the tone for everyone else in the organization, their role has the greatest impact in influencing the behaviors and attitudes of sales managers and employees alike. Great sales leaders know that everyone in their organization takes their cue from them as to what really matters. So they are clear when they want change, they know how to excite and inspire their organization, they make change personal, and they roll up their sleeves and get involved to help their teams deliver results.

Hubert Patricot

President, Europe, Coca-Cola Enterprises

How do you raise the bar on team performance?

Every spring, I go on a two-week tour along with our general managers. Each day we visit two cities in a country, but we only warn the local sales team 24 hours before our visit. Together with the local reps, we meet customers and discuss how we can improve our relationship. These impromptu visits help me assess first-hand the strengths of our business and challenge our teams on the ground. They also give me the opportunity to show my appreciation to our teams.

We also measure our progress and success with externally run surveys. We aspire to be the best, not just in the beverage sector but in the whole fast-moving consumer goods industry. We've achieved this in many European countries but I want all our countries to go for the top spot.

How do you excite and inspire your sales force?

Our Coca-Cola brand is exciting and our sales reps are passionate about selling our products. Major sponsorship deals help us create buzz among our sales teams. The World Cup or the London 2012 Olympics are great examples. We're recruiting young athletes training for the next Olympics to our sales team, and we ask them to talk to reps about their approach to preparing for the biggest event of their lives. The Olympic values of camaraderie, teamwork, and healthy competition excite our sales team and so we make the most out of these sponsored events to raise enthusiasm.

When do you get involved to make sure your team delivers growth?

As part of our annual sales planning, we look in detail at growth opportunities by segment, channel, and product lines, and develop specific sales action plans to capture growth. So, I make sure that our sales leaders deploy the 5,000 sales reps against these opportunities and make sure the leaders make the reps' lives easy so they can focus on selling. I also spend a lot of time in the field, sometimes even taking members of the board with me, to make sure that our "Coca-Cola Enterprises way" of selling is being used with every customer every time.

How do you develop sales leaders?

We take a holistic view of the competencies we want to see in sales leaders, based on our strategy. Our sales academy delivers these skills through a mix of on-the-job coaching, mentoring, and classroom style discussion. We combine this with 360-degree feedback focused on "leading to win". Finally, I spent a lot of my time mentoring our sales leaders.

What is your personal approach to leading your sales team?

I insist on team work every chance I have. Team work is essential in our business—we need perfect coordination between key account managers and local teams. To embed team work, I insist that high potential sales leaders spend time both with key accounts and in local sales positions during their career.

Perhaps most importantly, I try to make sure that our values—customer focus, team work, and accountability—guide my everyday decisions, as well as those of our 5,000 sales reps.

About the authors

Thomas Baumgartner

Thomas is a Director in the Vienna office of McKinsey & Company. He co-leads McKinsey's Global Sales & Channel service line. Thomas advises clients in industries such as high tech, electronics, transportation, basic materials, telecommunications, and consumer goods—where he helps his clients outline and drive large-scale top line growth programs. Over the last 10 years, he has led sales- and channel-related global research on topics such as the customer interaction model of the future, lean go-to-market, best-practice account management and winning in the small and medium segment. From 2004 to 2007 he was a university lecturer on global B2B marketing and sales. He holds a master and a doctorate degree in business administration from the University of Business Economics in Vienna.

Homayoun Hatami

Homayoun is a Principal in the Paris office of McKinsey & Company. He co-leads McKinsey's Sales Growth service line. He has a broad range of experience working with high-tech and telecommunications clients in Europe, the US, and Asia to help his clients drive growth. He was a member of the MIT Corporation (the board of trustees of the Massachusetts Institute of Technology) from 2001 to 2006. He received his Master of Science in computer science from Ecole Centrale Paris and his M.B.A. from the MIT Sloan School of Management, where he received the Seley Scholarship.

Jon Vander Ark

Jon is a Principal in McKinsey & Company's Detroit office. He co-leads McKinsey's Sales Growth service line. Jon has deep expertise in sales and channel management across industries including travel, automotive, industrial, and consumer durables. He is a frequent speaker on sales at industry forums and sales and marketing conferences. He has helped many industry leaders design and implement go-to-market strategies covering both direct and indirect channels. Jon received his B.A. from Calvin College and his J.D. from Harvard Law School.

Index

Account manager *see Sales force*
Account teams, 24
  see also *Key account management*
Analytical capabilities, 40, 131, 161
  granular insights, 42, 49

Best Buy, 139

Capability building, 6, 169–181
  coaching, 70, 158–160, 164
  experiential learning, 158, 173
  field and forum, 173
  hiring, 177–181
  role playing, 173
  sales managers as coaches, 159,
    164–165, 173, 175–177
Capital One, 130
Caterpillar, 106–109
Change management, 169–181
    culture, 172–175
    role of managers, 175–177
Channels, 57–109
  conflict, 102–104
  hybrid, 67, 69
  service channels, 69–71
  see also *Digital channels,*
    Direct channels, Indirect
    channels, Multichannel
Channel partners *see Indirect*
    channels
Churn, 133
Cisco, 134, 135

Close rate *see Win rate*
Coaching *see Capability building*
Coca-Cola Enterprises, 191–193
Commission *see Compensation*
Compensation, 87
    incentives/commission, 66, 159
    non-financial incentives, 98,
      162–163, 165–166
Consumer sales, 67, 82, 131, 137–140
  see also *Customer*
Cost of sales, 62–63, 82, 85, 94,
    97, 137
Customer
  acquisition, 87–88
  behavior, 24, 62–63, 74, 136, 142
  insights, 57–58, 77, 79, 138
  loyalty, 79–81, 124, 126–127, 166
  needs, 27, 78–80
  satisfaction, 59
  segmentation, 126, 133
  see also *Sales experience*
Customer service, 6, 121
  See also *Channels*

Demand
  investing ahead, 5, 23–35, 36–37
  modeling, 27, 32
Digital channels, 62, 67, 74, 103,
    137–140, 142–144
  mobile, 138–139
  social media, 138, 139–140
Direct channels, 68–69, 77–89,

conflict with indirect, 102–104
*see also Digital channels,
Sales force*
DuPont Pioneer, 51–53

EMC, 36–37
Emerging markets, 29, 75, 93, 186
Enterprise sales, 65, 102
Experts, 81–87, 135

Field reps *see Sales force*
Front line *see Sales force,
Sales managers*

Growth, 21, 37, 39–50
untapped pockets, 41–45, 51

Hiring *see Capability building*
Hunter-farmer model, 87, 88
Hybrid sales model *see Channels*
Hyundai, 26

IKEA, 67
Incentives *see Compensation*
Indirect channels, 68–69, 91–105,
106–109, 134, 135, 136,
brokers, 91–92
conflict with direct channels,
104–105, 185–186
dealer network, 29–31
loyalty, 98
performance management,
95–99, 102
see also Multichannel
Inside sales *see Sales force*
Internet *see Digital channels*

JCPenney, 67

Key account management, 85

Marketing budget, 46
Micro-markets, 39–50, 51–53
definition, 41
Middle managers *see Sales managers*
Mobile channels *see Digital channels*
Multichannel, 61–72, 73–75, 140,
185–186
channel conflict, 102–104
see also Channels

Online channel *see Digital channels*

Partners *see Indirect channels*
Performance management, 153–163,
164–166
dashboard, 154, 155
quotas, 69
reporting, 160–162, 165
ride-alongs, 159
sales planning, 154
targets, 174–175
*see also Capability building,
Compensation*
Phone sales *see Direct channels*
Pricing, 48
Product development, 77–78
lifecycle, 69

Retail stores, 42, 44, 73–74, 83–84
Routes to market *see Channels*

Sales collateral *see Sales tools*
Sales culture, 172–175
Sales experience, 57–59, 74–75,
137–140
Sales force, 169–181
attrition, 178, 180–181
coaching *see Capability building*
field reps, 47, 52, 65–66, 131
hiring, 177–181

inside sales/phone sales reps,
  65–66
productivity, 65, 119–121,
  154–155, 170–171
Sales leaders, 36–37, 51–53, 73–75,
  106–109, 142–144, 164–166,
  179–180, 183–190, 191–193
motivation, 186–187, 191–192
role models, 187–189
Sales/frontline managers, 174,
  175–177, 179–180
coaching see Capability building
Sales operations, 86, 92, 101, 115–127,
  135
back office, 116
colocation, 121
definition, 118
lean, 6
sales factories, 116
Sales pipeline, 45, 136
Sales tools, 166
collateral/support documents, 116
see also Technology-enabled sales
Salesforce.com, 14–144
Samsung, 73–75
SAP, 136
Small and mid-size customers, 66,
  93, 103
Social media see Digital channels
Specialists see Experts

Talent management see Capability
  building
TDC, 153–156, 157, 159–160, 176
Technology-enabled sales, 83,
  129–141,142–144
IT tools, 132–133
for indirect channels, 134
Telesales see Direct channels
Training see Capability building

Web see Digital channels
Win rate, 70, 80, 124, 160
Word of mouth, 80
Würth, 164–166